Design/Build

For Remodelers, Custom Builders, and Architects

Linda W. Case

Home Builder Press
National Association of Home Builders

Design/Build for Remodelers,
Custom Builders, and Architects

ISBN 0-86718-343-8
© 1989 by the National Association of Home Builders
of the United States

All rights reserved. No part of this book may be reproduced or utilized in any form or by any means, electronic or mechanical, including photocopying and recording or by any information storage and retrieval system without permission in writing from the publisher.

Printed in the United States of America

**Library of Congress
Cataloging-in-Publication Data**

Case, Linda W.
  Design/build for remodelers, custom builders, and architects / Linda W. Case.
     p. cm.
  Includes bibliographical references.
  ISBN 0-86718-343-8
  1. Construction industry—Customer services—Marketing.
2. Building trades—Customer services—Marketing. 3. House construction—Marketing. 4. Building—Marketing. 5. Dwellings Remodeling—Marketing. 6. Architecture, Domestic—Marketing.
  I. Title.
HD9715.A2C36   1989   90-5083
690′.068′8—dc20   CIP

For further information, please contact:

Home Builder Press
National Association of Home Builders
15th and M Streets, N.W.
Washington, D.C. 20005
(800) 223-2265

Publisher: Home Builder Press
National Association of Home Builders
Editor: Doris M. Tennyson
Art Director: David Rhodes

10/90 SCOTT/AUTOMATED

Contents

Acknowledgments ix

1. Introduction to Design/Build 1
The Remodeler 2
The Custom Home Builder 3
The Architect 4
The Bottom Line 5

2. The Design/Build Concept 7
The Concept 7
    The Free Introductory Stage 7
    The Design Phase 8
    The Construction Phase 8
Pros and Cons for the Professional 8
    Advantages for the Professional 8
        Reduces Competitive Bidding 8
        Works with the Serious Buyer 9
        Price/Budget Established Early 10
        Develops a Strong Working Relationship 10
        Sells Small Job, Then Big 10
        Improves Buildability of Plans 10
        Improves Accuracy of Estimating 11
        Receives Payment for Preparing Contract Documents 11
        Improves Ability To Assess On-Coming Work 11
        Increases Standardization 11
        Promotes Cohesive Design 12
        Increases Business Satisfaction 12
        Improves Firm's Image 12
        Simplifies Communication with Client 13
        Advantages Equal Control 13
    Disadvantages for the Professional 13
        Errors-and-Omissions Insurance 13
        Increased Legislation 14
        Need To Professionalize Design 15
        Increased Overhead and Business Complexity 15
        Increased Accountability 15
Pros and Cons for the Client 16
    Advantages for the Consumer 17
        Cost-Effective, Practical Construction 17
        One-Stop Shopping 18
        Customized, Professional Design 18
        Saves Time 20
        Provides Go or No-Go Stages 20
        Cohesiveness Between Design and Construction 20
        Saves Money on Design 20
        Strong Working Relationship 21
    Disadvantages of Design/Build for the Consumer 21
        Potential Conflict of Interest 21
        Lack of Competitive Construction Pricing 22
        Possible Lack of Insurance Coverage 22
        Potential Low-Quality Design 23
Seeing the Client's Perspective 23

3. Marketing Design/Build Services 25
Targeting Marketing Efforts 25
    Market Niche 26
    Company Image 27
    Community Image 28

Company-Generated Image   28
   Company Name   28
   Company Office Open to the Public   29
   Company Corporate Image Package   29
   Personnel Friendliness, Competence,
     Courteousness, and Dress   30
   Jobsite Appearance and Signage   30
   Vehicle Appearance and Signage   31
   Stationary Package   31
   Publicity and Advertising   32
Benefits of a Positive Image   34
Lead Generation   34
   Lead Quality   34
   Qualifying   34
   Lead Quantity   34
Marketing Indirectly to the Potential Client   35
   Marketing to the Former Client   36
   Developing Friends of the Company   38
   Positive Publicity   38
Marketing Directly to the Potential Client   40
    Success in Advertising   40
    Advertising Media   41
    Assessing an Advertising Medium   45
   Paying Commissions for Referrals   45
   Marketing and Selling from a Spec Home   46
Planning a Marketing Program   47
Keeping Marketing Statistics   48
Marketing as a Powerful Business Generator   48

4. Selling Design/Build Services   49
The Design/Build Salesperson   49
The Art of Selling   54
The Process   56
   Use of Letters   56
   Involving the Prospect   59
   The First Meeting   60
    Scope   60
    Budget   62
    Selling the Company   62
    Explaining Design/Build   64
    Setting the Next Appointment   64
   The Second Meeting   64
    Selling the Need for Design   65
    Selling Construction Services   68

5. The Design Phase   69
The Design Contract   70
Design Phase Stages   70
Designer Choices   74
   In-house Design   74
   Out-of-House Design   76
   Designer-Related Issues   76

Charging for Design   77
Ownership of Design   79
Estimating   79
Design Professionalism   81
Use of CAD   81
The Design Phase Menu   82
Interview with Tom Foley   82
   Resources   82

6. Contracts   83
Design Contracts   85
Construction Contract   85
   The Practical Construction Contract   89
    General Specifications   90
    General Conditions   91
    Ownership of Plans   92
    Defining Costs   93
    Rights of Cancellation and Recission   94
Reviewing the Contract with the Client   95
   Resources   95

7. Production of Design/Build Projects   97
Service Businesses   98
Transition from Sales to Production   101
Strong Field Leadership   101
   In-House Carpentry   103
   Improving Buildability   104
Strong Client Management   104
Site Walkthrough   105
Client Education   105
Product Selections   108
   Allowances for Product Selections   110
Client Changes   111
Design/Build's Impact on Production   111

8. Residential Design/Build for Remodelers   113
An Interview with David Johnston   115
   Company Profile   115
   Company History   115
   The Design/Build Process   115
    First Appointment   116
    The Design Contract   116
   Marketing   117
   Five-Year Plan   117
An Interview with Tom Mullen, CR   118
   Company Profile   118
   Company History   118
   Subcontracting Design   119
   The Design/Build Process   120
    The First Visit   120
    The Design Phase   120
   Construction   120
   Markup   120

Marketing   121
The Future   121

9. Design/Build for Custom Home Builders   123
An Interview with Tony Calvis   125
   Company Profile   125
   Company History   125
   Why Design/Build?   125
   Allowances   126
   Customer Relationships   126
   Marketing   127
   The Design/Build Process   127
      The Lead   127
      The First Meeting   127
      Lot Purchase   127
      Schematic Design   127
      Working Drawings   128
      Buildability   128
An Interview with Rick Jennings   129
   Company Profile   129
   Company History   129
   Design/Build in Custom Homes   129
   The Design/Build Process   129
      The Lead   129
      The First Visit   129
      The Second Visit   130
   Setting Budgets   130
   The Customer's Lot Selection   131
   Realtor Commissions   131
   Using Architects   131
   Design Liability   131
   The Team Approach   131
   Allowances   132
   Marketing   132
   Advantages of the Design/Build Niche   132
   Disadvantage of Design Build   132
An Interview with Bob Priest   133
   Company Profile   133
   Company History   133
   The Design/Build Process   133
      First Meeting   133
      Lot Search   134
      Conceptual Design   134
      The Decision Maker   134
      Working Drawings   134
      Budget   134
      Allowances   134
   Design Considerations   135
   Subcontractors   135
   Approved Suppliers   135
   Decorator Service   135
   On-Site Client Meetings   135
   Client Job Visits   135
   Client Changes   135

Marketing   136
Client Gifts   136

10. Residential Design/Build for Architects   137
An Interview with John Cable, AIA   139
   Company Profile   139
   Company History   139
   Managing the Design-Build Business   139
   Marketing   140
   The Design/Build Process   140
      The Lead   140
      The First Meeting   140
      Design Contract   141
      Design Schematics   141
      Cost Estimate   141
      Working Drawings   141
      Interface Between Production and Design   141
      The Construction Contract   142
An Interview with Walter Lynch   143
   Company Profile   143
   Company History   143
   The Design/Build Concept   143
   Marketing   143
   The Design/Build Process   144
      The Lead   144
      Design   144
      Client Budget   145
   Buildability of Plans   145
   Computer-Aided Design (CAD)   145
   The Client Relationship   145
   The Future   146

Design/Build Essentials Checklist   147
   Marketing   147
   Selling   147
   Designing   147
   Production   148

About the Author   149

Figures

Chapter 2. Concept
2-1. Pros and Cons from the Design/Builder's Perspective   9
2-2. Pros and Cons from the Client's Perspective   16
2-3. Consumer Advantages from Promotion Brochure   17

2-4. Consumer Advantages from Direct Mail Piece 19
2-5. Design/Build Description from Packet Sent to Leads 21

Chapter 3. Marketing Design/Build Services
3-1. Questions Design/Builders Use To Focus Their Marketing Programs 26
3-2. Page from Marketing Brochure 27
3-3. Interior of Design/Build Office 29
3-4. Office Sign 30
3-5. Logo 30
3-6. Postcard Sent to Jobsite Neighbors 31
3-7. Len McAdams and His Company Truck 31
3-8. Stationery Package 32
3-9. Inexpensive One-Color Brochure 33
3-10. Magazine-Style Brochure 33
3-11. Characteristics of a High-Quality Lead 35
3-12. Newsletter Produced by Design/Build Remodeling Firm 37
3-13. Reprint of Magazine Article 39
3-14. Criteria for Evaluating Lead-Generating Methods 41
3-15. Lead Producers 41
3-16. Newspaper Ad 42
3-17. Magazine Ad 43
3-18. Full-page Magazine Ad 43
3-19. *Yellow Pages* Ad 44
3-20. Tips for Assessing an Advertising Medium 45
3-21. Real Estate Flyer 46
3-22. Marketing Planning Tips 47

Chapter 4. Selling Design/Build Services
4-1. Example of Job Responsibilities and Performance Standards for a Salesperson-Designer 51
4-2. Developing a Presentation Book for Sales 55
4-3. Questions To Ask When Standardizing the Lead-Qualifying Process 56
4-4. Example of Sales Lead Report 57
4-5. Example of Initial Letter Responding to Lead 58
4-6. Example of Second Letter to Lead 58
4-7. Goals of the First Sales Meeting 59
4-8. Example of Homeowner Tips 61
4-9. Sample Checklist for the Design/Build Process 63
4-10. Goals of the Second and Third Sales Meetings 65
4-11. Sample Schematic of Office Addition 66
4-12. Sample Schematic of House Addition 67

Chapter 5. The Design Phase
5-1. Questions To Help a Design/Builder Organize the Design Phase 69
5-2. Sample Design/Build Schedule 71
5-3. Sample Schematic of House Addition 72
5-4. Sample Conceptual Design 73
5-5. Elements Provided by the Working Drawings 74
5-6. Sample Rendering of Custom Home 75
5-7. Sample Schedule of Fees 78
5-8. Sample Short Planning Estimate 80
5-9. Sample Title Block 81

Chapter 6. Contracts
6-1. Sample Design Contract 84
6-2. Elements To Be Included in a Design Contract 86
6-3. Sample Design and Drafting Agreement 87
6-4. Sample Design Contract 88
6-5. Twelve Ways to Prevent Liability Problems 89
6-6. Contract Clauses That Need Customizing 90
6-7. Contract Clauses That Can Be Standard for All Projects 90
6-8. Standard Specification Items 91
6-9. Items Usually Covered in General Conditions 92
6-10. Requirement of the Right of Rescission 95

Chapter 7. Production of Design/Build Projects
7-1. Design/Build Advantages for Production 97
7-2. Memo of Instructions to Subcontractors 99
7-3. Sample Job Folder Checklist 102
7-4. Tips for Design/Build Cost Control 103
7-5. Job Work Rules 104
7-6. Sample Design/Build Site Checklist 106
7-7. Sample Design/Build Selection 109
7-8. Sample Entry for Client's Selection 110

Chapter 8. Residential Design/Build for Remodelers
8-1. David Johnston and Eric Havens 115
8-2. Magazine Article Reprint and Promotion Piece 116
8-3. The Johnston/Havens Philosophy 117
8-4. Tom Mullen 118
8-5. Letterhead Conveys Design/Build Niche 119
8-6. The Mullen Philosophy 121

Chapter 9. Design/Build for Custom Home Builders
9-1. Characteristics of Successful, Design/Build Custom Builders 124
9-2. Tony Calvis 125

9-3. The Stationery Package Promotes Custom Design, Building, and Remodeling 126
9-4. The Calvis Philosophy 128
9-5. Rick Jennings, Judy Nichols, Mark Pemperton 129
9-6. Foil-Stamped Stationery Package Attracts Luxury Market 130
9-7. The Jennings Philosophy 132
9-8. Bob Priest 133
9-9. A Custom Home by Bob Priest 134
9-10. The Priest Philosophy 136

Chapter 10. Residential Design/Build for Architects
10-1. John Cable 139
10-2. Advertisement Based on Jobsite Sign and Logo 140
10-3. The Cable Philosophy 142
10-4. Walter Lynch 143
10-5. Rendering of a Custom Home 144
10-6. The Lynch Philosophy 145

Acknowledgements

Design/Build for Remodelers, Custom Builders, and Architects is rooted in the generosity of the design/builders who interrupted their daily work and shared their hard won secrets. Why did they share what others might protect? Because they had an industry-wide loyalty and put great stock in helping others to avoid the pitfalls that "inventing the wheel" creates. They were only too ready to provide a form, a brochure, a method, or a philosophy. So if you gain by using this book, thank your brothers and sisters in construction and pass on what you have learned to others.

Thanks are also due to the following reviewers whose suggestions improved the ideas and methods presented here: Robert Hall, chairman, NAHB Single Family Custom Building Committee, and president, RH Building Contractors Inc., Sarasota, California; Glenn Sims, president, Glenn Sims Remodeling Company, Tucker, Georgia; and Ron Nickson, NAHB construction technology and codes specialist.

I also thank Mary Dicrescenzo, NAHB associate litigation counsel, for her review of Chapter 6, "Contracts," and the "Increasing Legislation" section in Chapter 2, "The Design/Build Concept," and Lloyd Unsell, NAHB insurance specialist, for reviewing the "Errors and Omissions" section of that same chapter.

The inspired design by David Rhodes, art director, NAHB Home Builder Press, makes the contents of the book both easily accessible and attractive.

The unseen, unsung person behind this book is its editor, Doris M. Tennyson, director, special projects/senior editor, NAHB Home Builder Press. This is the third book on which we have comfortably collaborated. If you find it easy to read, flowing in its concepts, pleasing to the eye, that's because Doris has been working unstintingly on your behalf.

Linda W. Case, CRA

1

Introduction to Residential Design/Build

When design/build is done well, it involves the packaging of high-quality, professional design services with high-quality, professional construction services. Charging the client a fee for each phase is inherent in design/build. For the remodeler, custom builder, and architect, design/build represents an operating style and a service mode that is closely in tune with what today's client wants—a seamless, cost-effective, functional project from one accountable source.

Remodelers and custom home builders have long recognized that plans were necessary to sell their jobs. In the past, those plans were often done free of charge. Because they were free, not enough time may have been spent to assure customer satisfaction. Overall quality of design often suffered. The design was simply a sketchy facilitator that (a) allowed the builder or the remodeler to obtain permits and (b) provided just enough information to give the client a rough idea of what was included in the contract.

During the 1970s the concept of residential design/build started to become a trend. By the late 1980s many customers were beginning to recognize the term and to ask for the packaging of services it represented. The 1990s may well make design/build the operational mode of choice for remodelers and custom home builders.

The concept involves nothing new or radical. Early builders were often designers and vice versa. In medieval times, for example, the guild craftsmen were directed by the master mason who functioned much like today's designer/builder. He not only designed the structure by sketching his plans on parchment, he also managed the construction.

The demographics of today's population might give some clues

> *The implications are clear. Whether you're married, a single parent, or a single person, most households today are made up of people who are working a lot and who have multiple obligations. This translates into pressure and a high-stress consumer environment. Anything that relieves that pressure, even for a moment, is going to be appreciated.*
>
> —Martha Farnsworth Riche
> American Demographics, Inc.[1]

as to why the buyer has embraced this new-old design/construction packaging:

- The consumer is time poor. Because of the increased frequency of two working spouses, today's buyer is looking for ways to simplify the purchasing of services and products.
- The increased stress on the quality of the home environment seems to be in inverse proportion to the time spent there. Many more meals are eaten out or carried in and yet the kitchen has never been more important in terms of size and style. Look at the trend toward huge master baths and bedroom suites, great rooms, and multiple fireplaces—all at a time when the family members are decreasingly at home.
- The ability to create a one-of-a-kind customized home environment through custom homebuilding or remodeling of existing space is highly valued. It is the ultimate "yuppie" status symbol.

Thus, design/build is an operating style that fits the times. One-stop shopping, one-stop accountability, functional and cost-efficient design are highly valued by today's consumer. How does design/build fit the remodeler, builder, or architect? It's a win-win operating style.

The Remodeler

In remodeling, design/build has proven to be tremendously liberating for the remodeler as well as a highly useful service for the buyer. It truly represents a win-win solution for both parties. Plans are required for virtually all remodeling jobs: to communicate with the client, to instruct carpenters and subcontractors about the scope of the work, and often, to obtain local building permits. Historically, these plans were free and were developed as part of the selling process.

If the prospects did not buy—and often they did not—the plans and the time spent to develop them were lost. To add insult to injury, the client often took the relatively professional set of plans and shopped them with less expensive and less creative contractors.

Many remodelers depend on architects to design their remodeling projects and generate their business. The consumer decides he/she wants to remodel a home and starts by contracting with an architect to design that remodeling. Often budget is discussed, and the design attempts to meet that budget.

Once plans are complete either the consumer or the architect looks for a contractor to construct the project. The remodeler who seeks this type of work is now put in a bidding position where selection could be based on price alone. Little opportunity is available to make a case for value over price. Therefore, a high-quality company has difficulty surviving when low price is the selection criteria. Many remodelers have moved from this arena into design/build. Ironically enough, some remodelers now

> *We have always provided plans for our clients, but design/build is an evolution—a next step—to professionalize our process and charge for it.*
>
> —Tim Fleming, remodeler
> Arlington, Virginia.

subcontract their designs to those same architects for whom they used to bid.

Remodelers who have used design/build in their approach for a number of years tend to charge 3 to 4 percent of the gross budget and generally produce a professional set of blueprints. Obviously, remodelers who have a well-developed sense of design and creative flair are the most likely to be attracted to this operating mode.

Remodeling is likely to be a hot construction market in the 1990s with an anticipated national volume of $108 billion in 1990 of which approximately 75 percent will be professionally installed.[2] The annual growth rate is projected at 3 to 4 percent per year over the 1990s. In 1990 remodeling is expected to represent 48 percent of all residential construction, and by 1993, residential remodeling will probably be as large as new home construction.[3]

A 1987 NAHB study showed that 70 percent of remodelers offer in-house design services,[4] but that not all charge fees for those services.

Informal estimates suggest that 20 percent of full-line residential remodelers over $1 million in volume probably operate as design/build firms as well as probably 5 percent of companies under $1 million in residential full-line remodeling.

The Custom Home Builder

Builders have been doing design/build for years but didn't have a name for it.

—Rick Jennings, custom home builder
Ormond Beach, Florida

For the purposes of this book, a custom home builder is defined as building a one-of-kind home for a client. In recent years the tendency is to extend the term, *custom builder*, to all builders of upper-end homes even if they are not presold. However, design/build always presupposes a client.

The custom home builder has been in essentially the same position as the residential remodeler. Such a builder had to develop the plans needed for building the custom house, but those blueprints were often just a free part of the selling process to attract the consumer into a construction contract. Some custom home builders found themselves in a bidding war with other builders for architecturally designed plans.

An operating system that allows the beleaguered custom home builder to work on a professional level with a serious client without constant price pressure has been well received, and many custom builders now operate as design/build firms. Because design/build is seen as basically a marketing tool, custom home builders and remodelers are inclined to refund part of the design fee if the client signs a construction contract. This practice signifies that they view design as a marketing "chute" into what they really want—the construction project. However, the design process can be a profit center within the company. Costs and revenue can be tracked through job costs.

The Economics and Housing Policy Department of the National Association of Home Builders reports that housing units built on client-owned land numbered as follows in the years listed below:

Year	Custom-Built Units
1986	204,000
1987	208,000
1988	196,000
1989	192,000

The custom homebuilding market is considered stable yet flat in its growth.

The Architect

For the architect, design/build is also a liberating advance. Prior to 1978 the American Institute of Architects (AIA) had banned architects from building the projects they had designed. At the 1978 AIA Convention, a resolution allowing design/build for architects narrowly passed, but only on an experimental basis. Later regulation and litigation made design/build an acceptable combination for architects.

Architects find the combination of design and construction allows for a larger sale to the same client with a much larger base for profit. Being able to sell more than just design hours—including the labor, materials, and subcontractors involved with the construction package—has opened new business opportunities for architects.

In the past many architects refused to design a remodeling project or single house because of the difficulty in charging adequately for the time-intense, one-of-a-kind design and customer service that was required. Design/build creates a critical business mass for an architectural firm.

Another important drawing card for the architect is the opportunity to assure design consistency throughout the process. Involvement with the job throughout construction should result in a seamlessly designed and constructed project.

The American Institute of Architects estimates that 10 to 12 percent of architects are engaged in design/build. This percentage is likely to increase. As a group, architects are well-suited to design-build because they tend to be extremely client-oriented and fairly relaxed about how much time is spent in the design process. They usually view design as a profit center and make money on it. Normally, architects do not refund design monies if clients continue into construction with their firms.

I was sure I had a marketable niche by combining my design expertise and construction ability. Frankly, I thought this was a fairly unique idea. I didn't know I was part of a trend.

—John Cable, AIA, architect
Alexandria, Virginia

I was attracted to the total design/construction package. The architecture is what I enjoy, but the construction is where the real money is.

—Walter Lynch, architect
Arlington, Virginia

The Bottom Line

Design and construction are one continuous process and that process is successful when the client is left happy.

—David Johnston, remodeler
Bethesda, Maryland

Design/build provides a profitable operating style in the residential construction market. No longer a trend to be watched, design/build is one to consider joining. It is a solidly established way to improve selling and working conditions for numerous remodelers, architects, and custom home builders. Businesspeople working in the residential market should know and understand design/build as well as the critical factors for successfully converting to this important service.

Design/Build for Remodelers, Custom Builders, and Architects focuses on the advantages and disadvantages of this service, how to market and sell the package, how to make designs sell construction for the company, as well as how design/build impacts production. This book tells experienced design/builders how to glean more benefits (and more profits) from this mode of operation, and it guides beginners safely past many of the potential problems.

To some degree, the design/build mode of operation represents only a small shift from the traditional approach of free plans for everyone who may buy a construction job. But, as subsequent chapters will show, marketing, selling, and producing design/build jobs involve many important nuances.

The final three chapters primarily include interviews with seven successful design/builders (remodelers, custom builders, and architects who are practitioners of design/build). The interviews examine where they began, how they operate today, and what road led between those two points.

Notes

1. Presentation for the National Kitchen and Bath Association, April 13, 1988, New York City.
2. "State of the Remodeling Industry," *Remodeling*, Washington, D.C., 1989, p. 7.
3. "State of the Remodeling Industry," p. 1.
4. *1987 Profile of the Remodeler and His Industry* (Washington, D.C.: National Association of Home Builders, 1987), p. 49.

2

The Design/Build Concept

Offering either design services or construction services to the public is not unusual. However, design/build is a case of 1 plus 1 equals more than 2. When a custom builder, remodeler, or architect combines both services into one company, consumers perceive and actually receive greater functional value. Experts say a product or service sells only two ways: either it must sell based on low price or on a differentiation of features. Architects, custom builders, and remodelers offering design/build services are virtually never inexpensive. They have chosen to sell their services based on value-added features and the potent combination of those two services.

The Concept

Design/build firms sprouted independently around the country, but successful practitioners (design-builders) have remarkably similar operating styles. They may add a step or delete a phase, but their selling, designing, and production follows the basic, three-part pattern explored in depth throughout this book and described briefly in the paragraphs that follow.

The Free Introductory Stage

When the potential client or lead calls to inquire about the design/builder's services, the person taking the call asks a number of informational and qualifying questions, including budget range. If the caller appears to be a good candidate for the design/builder's services, a first appointment is scheduled. For the remodeler, this first appointment should be scheduled to take place in the client's home because the existing space will have tremendous impact on what can be added.

For the custom home builder, the first appointment can be either at his/her office or at the client's home. This first meeting is to qualify the potential buyer's likelihood and ability to build, to discuss scope, and to delineate at least a rough budget. Usually at a second free visit, the budget range is confirmed, perhaps some simple, selling-type schematics are reviewed, and the custom home builder suggests that the prospective buyer move into the design phase.

For architects, who are traditionally used to giving only one free meeting, this initial free stage may well be compressed to one visit.

The Design Phase
Traditionally design has been broken into three stages—schematics, design development, and working drawings. Most design/builders follow some such method of zeroing in on final decision-making by the client. This stage may take 1 to 3 months depending on the complexity of the job, the traffic in the design department, and the needs of both the design/builder and the client.

The Construction Phase
A relatively seamless move into construction takes place within the design/build process, but often a delay occurs between the two while the company secures permits and completes its production package.[1]

The Pros and Cons for the Professional

When a company takes the design/build road, certain doors or options are opened and others are closed. Design/build has tradeoffs—advantages and disadvantages—for both the design/builder and the consumer (Figure 2-1).

Advantages for the Professional

The advantages of working as a design/build firm are overwhelming. They tip the odds in the builder's and remodeler's favor. In one area after another—marketing, selling, designing, estimating, production, client relations—design/build liberates the practitioners and provides a much more favorable working climate in which their firms can flourish.

Reduces Competitive Bidding
Probably the single most important advantage of design/build is that it tends to eliminate most competitive bidding. A custom builder, remodeler, or architect may take a few years to refine the system, but most firms find they do little bidding against other companies. In fact, once design/build is established, the firm frequently declines to do any competitive bidding. This allows the design/builder to set a realistically fair markup and stick with it.

The reason bidding is eliminated is that the consumer and design/builder set a budget range initially before the design contract is signed. The consumer is basically saying that if the firm can design the project within the prospect's budget, the prospect will move

> **Figure 2-1. Pros and Cons from the Design/Builder's Perspective**
>
> **Advantages of Design/Build**
> - Reduces competitive bidding
> - Enables the design/builder to work with the serious buyer
> - Helps to establish budget/price early
> - Develops a strong, healthy working relationship between the parties during design phase
> - Sells a small job to gain a big sale later
> - Improves buildability of plans
> - Improves accuracy of estimating
> - Allows the design/builder to obtain payment for preparing plans and contract documents
> - Improves ability to assess the level of on-coming work
> - Increases standardization of products and building systems
> - Promotes cohesive design
> - Increases business satisfaction
> - Improves the firm's image
> - Improves communication with client
> - Provides greater control over entire project
>
> **Disadvantages of Design/Build**
> - Involves difficult to obtain and costly errors-and-omission insurance
> - Increases the amount of restrictive regulation with which the firm must deal (concerning design)
> - Creates need to professionalize design services
> - Increases overhead and business complexity
> - Increases accountability

directly into construction. The stages of the design/build process do not provide a convenient time or cogent reason to stop to competitively bid the project as long as budget integrity is maintained and a strong working relationship develops. Without budget control and a strong working relationship design/build will not work.

Works with the Serious Buyer
While most companies offer a free first and second visit to the potential client, that is normally the extent of time given away without charge. At the end of the second visit, the client must decide whether to sign a design contract.

These initial visits delineate the scope of the job, define a realistic budget range, and help both parties become comfortable with one another. In order to continue further, the prospective customer must pay for design. The customer is asked to commit to a design

After all, if I couldn't get the customers to pay for the plans, I knew I couldn't get them to sign a construction contract.

—Tom Mullen, CR, remodeler
Scottsdale, Arizona

fee. It is a small-ticket sale—perhaps $750 to $5,000, but it shows that the client is committed to proceeding with the project. This signing of a design contract is a heavy qualifier. It signifies that the client is a serious buyer for the entire project.

Price/Budget Established Early
For construction clients, the design stage should be a pleasant phase. Production is the stage that exerts stress on clients. But even design has the "downer" of the final price. Conversation to that point has been animated, dreams have been discussed, family aspirations drawn and quantified, but great tension still rides on the pricing that usually concludes this phase. Will the two parties build together? That question is not settled until the price is given by the builder and accepted by the prospective client.

When the design/build process is not followed, the contractor and prospective client cannot and do not establish a close working relationship because once the price is on the table, the client may decide to go with another contractor's bid.

Design/build sweeps that tension away by establishing budget range at the second visit. At the point the client decides to move ahead into design, the contractor, figuratively moves over to the client's side of the table and becomes guardian of the budget and fulfiller of dreams. If the process is running properly, no "surprises" develop, and the relationship runs smoothly.

Develops a Strong Working Relationship
Because the contractor and client anticipate a seamless design-construction process, they will automatically begin to work together—to learn each other's operating style. This "honeymoon" occurs during the pleasant stage of design. An excellent working relationship should blossom during this stage to carry the parties through production. However, if serious frictions are present, both parties have an opportunity to back out of the relationship.

Sells Small Job, Then Big
Design/build provides a tremendous selling opportunity. Instead of trying to make an $85,000 addition sale after meeting potential clients a few times, the remodeler can focus on selling a $1,500 to $2,000 design for an addition.

However, the experienced design/build firm anticipates converting 80 to 90 percent of those small design sales into construction project sales. When that conversion does not occur, usually either the client's budget has been exceeded or a strong, trustful, working relationship has not developed.

Improves Buildability of Plans
Ask builders and remodelers about architecturally designed work, and they often complain that the drawings were underdetailed or basically unbuildable. When a company functions as a design/build firm, it has no excuse for underdetailed or unbuildable plans.

> *All the communication between owner and architect and contractor is simply aimed at the craftsperson being able to do the job.*
>
> —Tim Pleune, remodeler
> Denver, Colorado

Ensuring buildability and transferring clear information to the field is controlled by the design/builder. Established design/build companies focus on this tremendous opportunity to save money and to smooth out company operations.

Improves Accuracy of Estimating

Because the design/builder is working intimately with the plans from first schematics through conceptual drawings to the final working drawings, he/she is constantly exposed to estimating as the project develops. The design/builder may run two to four estimates—one at each stage—as part of the budget-guardian role so that scope and budget are brought into line. Constant familiarity with specifications contrasts sharply with bidding an outside set of blueprints on which the deadline for bid submission might be only 2 weeks. The design/builder may have 2 to 3 months to price the job out completely, to meet subcontractors at the site, and to receive careful estimates from suppliers.

Receives Payment for Preparing Contract Documents

Design/builders frequently make the design fee cover just the actual cost of the design phase. Most custom builders and remodelers who move into design/build set that goal. After years of giving away design, they are more than content to at least trade dollars, but they can make it into a profit center. Architects who move into the design/build mode tend to keep their orientation toward making money on design and use it as one of their two profit centers—with construction as the second center.

Under either philosophy, the client is not only paying for the design preparation time but also for estimating time as well as the considerable hours needed to prepare specifications and contract documents. For the remodeler and custom home builder who have been used to paying for these stages as overhead, this feature of design/build is a true advantage.

Improves Ability To Assess On-Coming Work

Design/builders know their conversion rates from design contracts to construction contracts range from 80 to 90 percent, so they can anticipate their workloads for a longer time period. For example, company A's projects stay in design an average of 2 months, and the company has a 92 percent conversion rate. If the firm has $1.5 million under design, the design/builder can anticipate $1.4 million in work moving into construction within the next 2 months. By the same token, the longer process inherent in design/build allows the company to speed up or slow work to feed it into construction at an appropriate speed depending on workload conditions.

Increases Standardization

Design/build presents an opportunity for dollar savings and efficiency in estimating and production. Because the builder controls the design, standard products and building systems can be specified. Only when the client does not want what the builder/remodeler normally provides, is that standard changed. In this way, clients get exactly what they want, at the same time that the design/builders achieve an increasing level of standardization.

Successful design/builders estimate that 90 percent of the products and 95 percent of the building systems in a project will remain as specified by the design/builder. In fact, the clients are seeking just such guidance from design/builders. Which windows are good quality, stylish, locally stocked, and well warranted? The professional should be able to bring that information to the table.

To make full use of this advantage, design/builders need to carefully choose their products considering both sales and production needs. The salesperson wants a brand he/she can readily sell, some snazzy features, high-quality brochures and specification sheets, and a competitive price. The production manager wants to be able to buy a product quickly and reliably in the local market, install it easily, and have support from the distributors in case of a problem.

Standardization increases the efficiency of designing for in-house production. Much detailing may be omitted if it is the standard company detailing. The designer knows exactly what is needed to communicate to the company's carpenters. If unknown framing subcontractors are to be used for a project, the company will have to return to more detailed plans and specifications.

Promotes Cohesive Design

A number of design decisions are made after plans are completed, and the job is in production. The client inevitably makes changes. Existing conditions may impact a remodeling design. Design/builders enjoy their ability to redesign as needed in keeping with the original vision of the job. Architect design/builders frequently mention this advantage. Architects who do design-only—and do not have supervision of a job—are often jarred by the changes that are made to their designs by builders.

Increases Business Satisfaction

Builders and remodelers often have considerable design talent. Because of the nature of the businesses they are in, many are interested in and value excellent design. At the same time, many architects would like to be involved in the construction of the job—actually turning the abstract plan into the concrete project. For many architects, custom builders, and remodelers, design/build is not only the smart way to do business but the fun way.

Improves Firm's Image

Public image sometimes places the designer of a building or remodeling job in the white-collar, professional category. Sadly, some clients see the builder or remodeler of that same project as a service person or technician. With some clients, the "professional" may have greater credibility and be used on a more consultative

---

Because of the closer relationship between architect and builder who are working together on a design/build project, design changes are addressed more sensitively. Design/build does help to extend design continuity throughout the project.

—Bruce Wentworth, architect forming a design/build company with a remodeler
Washington, D.C.

> *Many design/build contractors experience much greater job satisfaction, since their expertise is valued on a much grander scale. Creative involvement, combined with the actual construction, offers a tremendous sense of accomplishment.*[2]
> —Michael M. Milliner, commercial design/builder
> Frederick, Maryland

basis. The combination of services should allow the design/builders to take advantage of the professional nature of this role as more of a helpful consultant and be treated by their clients as such.

Simplifies Communication with Client

Every architect, builder, and remodeler who has worked on a project in which the three parties—client, architect, and contractor—have a major interest but are not pulling as a team, understands how the elimination of one party will streamline the process. The potential for disagreement and blaming are reduced. The client and design/builder settle what needs to be settled more easily.

In addition, when the designer and builder or remodeler are the same person, any changes can be made more expeditiously because only two parties need to discuss the change—the client and the design/builder.

Advantages Equal Control

Many of the advantages (discussed in the preceding paragraphs) that result from adopting a design/build service strategy hinge on control—control of the client, control of the process, control of products and building systems. The design/builder or remodeler is not looking to be a dictator but merely to weight the odds in his/her favor.

Disadvantages for the Professional

Design/build may be a liberation for the remodeler, builder, and or an architect, but it is not without its disadvantages. Some of these drawbacks are both major and intractable.

Errors-and-Omissions Insurance

While the architect may be fully aware that this design malpractice insurance is needed to cover design failures, the remodeler and builder may not. If a beam is incorrectly sized on the plans and a structural failure occurs because of that design error, the resulting costs to rebuild are not covered under a construction liability policy. This critical gap in the insurance coverage of most design/build firms creates an extreme disadvantage.

Only a few insurance carriers issue errors-and-omissions insurance, the annual cost is extremely expensive, and the insurance carriers are choosy about which companies they cover. They tend to frown on design/build companies because the two professional specialties are supplied by the same company rather than by two independent parties that might scrutinize each others work more carefully.

For these reasons, design/builders often do not carry this vital insurance coverage. Custom builders and remodelers often commit to designing conservatively and call in registered architects and engineers on an as-needed basis for consultation. When using such consultants, these two types of firms should be sure to inquire whether the consultants carry such professional liability coverage and, if so, request a certificate of insurance.

Design/builders need to consider developing an agreement with these outside consultants in which they hold the design/build firm harmless for any damage their consultations may cause. These suggestions only mitigate exposure; they do not correct it. Every design/build firm should focus on this dangerous exposure and take every available remedy to keep it as small as possible. They should be sure to consult with an attorney and a well-trained insurance agent as to how the company should handle this insurance problem.

Increased Legislation
As design/build becomes a more popular operating style for custom building and remodeling contractors, it is likely to prompt attempts to pass more restrictive legislation to limit the ability to offer design services without a registered or licensed architect on staff.

Closely allied to lack of errors-and-omission insurance is the disadvantage that many states throughout the country do not have a statute of limitations on design errors.

Registered architects (licensed by the state) have professional liability. They are charged with protecting the health, safety, and welfare of those in and around their buildings regardless of what the client or the builder requests. They cannot protect themselves from this liability by incorporating as an architectural nor as a design/build firm.

Under many state laws, the terms, *architect*, *architectural plans*, *architectural services*, possibly even the terms, *designer* and *design*, by a design/builder may indicate that the design/ builder (a) is practicing architecture, (b) is offering to practice architecture, or (c) that he/she is a licensed architect. In other words, design/builder's use of these words may be restricted in advertising, in conversations with clients, and in the daily conduct of their businesses. Therefore, all design/builders and remodelers should research whether they are subject to such regulations.

Anyone considering moving into the design/build mode of operation must first find out how the state in which he/she plans to operate defines the practice of architecture. The design/builder needs to check that definition, especially for the work that can only be done by an architect and for what that state considers practicing architecture without a license.

This definition varies from state to state. Some states define the practice of architecture in such a way that it encompasses typical design/build services, and some do not. Some states' definitions of the practice of architecture do not restrict design/build, but they have an additional law that specifically requires a design/builder to have an architect on the staff. In either case, to comply with the law, a design/builder would have to either (a) limit the services provided to the type of work specifically exempted under his/her

> *Please be advised that any unlicensed person who advertises in a manner so as to indicate that such a person is an architect or offers to provide architectural services is in violation of N.J.S.A. 45:3-10. The use of words or phrases such as design, designer, design and construction, design and planning services and similar wording in connection with building advertisements implies an offer to provide architectural services.*
>
> —A cease-and-desist order from the New Jersey State Board of Architects to a design/build remodeler

state's regulation of the practice of architecture or (b) have an architect on the staff.

Sometimes design/builders have had registered architects and engineers review and "stamp" the plans so that they will pass state regulations. This practice is illegal in many states, and any regulations regarding the practice should be carefully researched and strictly followed.

Need To Professionalize Design

Builders and remodelers should anticipate that making a transition to design/build will involve more than just "business as usual" with a change from free design to charging for design. Clients who are willing to pay for design, value it and want it to be at a professional level. For many remodelers and builders this requirement means a definite upgrade in the quality of the planning and the presentation of the plans as well as in the plans themselves. Drafting skills, lettering, title blocks all need to be professional. When clients understand the enhanced value of professional design and are willing to pay for it, among other things, these clients also want—

- The luxury of spending more time in the design phase
- Skillful delineation of their needs by the design/builder
- A number of planning options from which to choose

The design phase will be considerably longer and more service oriented than when free plans were quickly generated as a facilitator to construction. For architects, this disadvantage does not exist because they are trained to work at a professional design level and expect to provide that paid-for service.

Increased Overhead and Business Complexity

In moving into design/build, the remodeler and custom builder must add design services, and the architect must expand into construction services. While those additional services are sometimes provided through subcontracting or joint venture, they are most frequently added in-house. Because of these additions, the companies involved must support personnel who, at least in the beginning, may not be fully occupied and paid for by services delivered. In a downturn the company may need to carry more personnel than it otherwise would in order to provide design/build services when needed.

Design/build also adds to the complexity of the business because the firm must deliver another major service in a professional manner. For a company to be top quality in both design and construction is difficult—but that is what today's market demands.

Increased Accountability

Because the design/builder has controlled and provided the entire spectrum of services on a particular job, all blame for what is not designed well or crafted well falls on his/her shoulders. The other company or professional that might have shared the blame is now part of the same firm.

Savvy design/builders stay fully aware and up-to-date on these disadvantages. They take all precautions to minimize the downside and maximize the advantages. Most design/builders ultimately decide that the advantages far outweigh the drawbacks.

Pros and Cons for the Client

Design/build is a win-win operating style for both the professional and the client. The advantages for both outweigh the negatives. When astute design/builders sell design/build, they are prepared to meet and respond to the disadvantages when prospective clients raise them as objections to the sale. When design/builders fully understand these objections, they can deal with them in the selling process.

In general, clients could go the free-plan route, especially in remodeling, or they might choose to work with the architect or designer for the design services (and possibly construction supervision) and then hire a remodeler or builder to do the construction. Design/build must meet or beat these other options in order to be sellable (Figure 2-2).

Figure 2-2. Pros and Cons from the Client's Perspective

Advantages of Design/Build for the Consumer
- Provides cost-effective practical construction
- Provides one-stop shopping and accountability
- Customized, professional design adds value to a home
- Design/build saves time from concept to completion
- Design/build provides a number of go or no-go stages
- Design/build facilitates cohesiveness between design and construction
- Design is achieved more economically
- Design/build offers the client a chance to develop a solid working relationship with the design/builder before signing the construction contract

Disadvantages of Design/Build
- Potential for conflict of interest (because one independent professional is eliminated)
- Lack of competitive construction pricing
- Possible lack of full insurance coverage
- Potential for lower quality of design

Advantages for the Consumer

Design/build offers a variety of advantages to the consumer. Those clients value most are discussed in the paragraphs below.

Cost-Effective, Practical Construction

The single most important reason a consumer should consider a design/build firm is that the design/builder has all the expertise in-house to design and construct to a specified budget. Guarding the client's budget requires day-in, day-out estimating, purchasing, and assessing actual job costs for a firm to be able to match scope to budget. Unless a consumer has an unlimited budget, this careful and knowledgeable adherence to budget is critical (Figure 2-3).

Figure 2-3. Consumer Advantages from Promotion Brochure

Modern Design/Build process Reduces Time, Cost, and Headaches for Homeowners.

The home remodeling industry, an $80 billion dollar annual business, has surprisingly few professionally-run contractors involved. According to the Better Business Bureau, complaints against remodeling contractors rank second only to complaints against used car dealers. The problems usually involve unfulfilled promises, projects over budget, and shoddy workmanship.

A primary basis for distinction in the Merrill approach is the design/build process. The firm can identify the concerns of the clients and the goals of the project, and then participate in the design process and produce specifications to meet both client needs _and_ budget. Prior to costly architectural design fees for finished plans, the basic design and scope of work is laid out and "estimated." Using the design/build system, adjustments may be made prior to commiting to a finished set of blueprints, saving time and costly re-drafting fees.

In contrast, many contractors will require the client to pay an architect or designer for a complete set of plans before the budget has really been established. It is common knowledge that only one out of three of those designs even gets built as drawn!

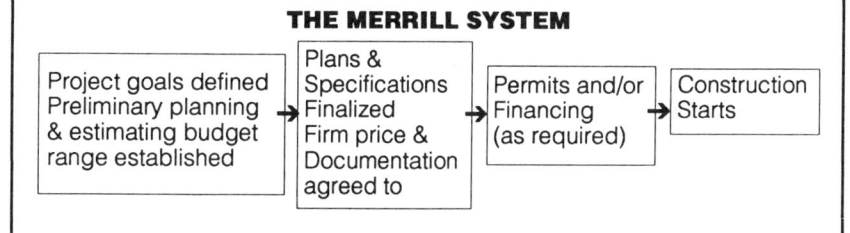

THE MERRILL SYSTEM

Project goals defined Preliminary planning & estimating budget range established → Plans & Specifications Finalized Firm price & Documentation agreed to → Permits and/or Financing (as required) → Construction Starts

---

Source: Reprinted with permission from Jim Merrill, president, Merrill Home Remodeling, The JR Merrill Group, Renton, Washington.

> *As a design/build firm, we're not oriented toward monuments to our design nor toward architectural statements. We really try to meet the client's needs in a way that is harmonious with the existing house and the available budget.*
>
> —David Johnston, remodeler
> Bethesda, Maryland

Additionally, when the company designing the project is also the construction company, design is likely to be more buildable and that means more cost effective. The construction company knows what products work well, have reliable warranties and are available locally for competitive prices. Design/builders are much less likely to design monuments to themselves because they would have to build them, and such structures would be costly and difficult to build.

One-Stop Shopping

Today's consumers are time poor. Time, not money, is their most precious commodity. In fact this consumer market has been called the "Do It for Me" (DIFM) market. They are attracted to a business that will take care of everything related to a project. They want to work with a builder or remodeler who will run with their ideas, come back with suggestions and selections, and ultimately, present them with a finished product.

They are also attracted to the concept of one accountable expert, so that, if they are concerned with any detail or execution of that detail, handling the problem does not get tied up in finger pointing between experts. Instead they only have to deal with one business that stands behind its work.

Customized, Professional Design

Three socioeconomic groups—the middle class, the upper middle class, the wealthy—are potential consumers of design/build services. The most receptive socioeconomic group for design/build is the upper middle class. In fact, design/build should be considered primarily an upper middle-class niche demographically. However, design/build also serves the wealthy.

Because the members of the truly wealthy class—a tiny slice of the population pie—normally buy from "the expert" in each area, they are often attracted to working with an architect. They want a one-of-a-kind, highly customized design. By using an architect, they can make sure they will not see their custom homes or additions repeated elsewhere in their neighborhoods. Therefore, they provide a fertile market for the architect design/builder because they value design credentials highly. Wealthy prospects will be much less attracted to the remodeler or builder who may not have an architect on staff and who may be seen as not producing state-of-the-art design.

In contrast, the members of the middle class have fewer discretionary dollars and tend to see less value added by design, so design/build may be less attractive to them. They like brand names in products and often are happy for their houses or additions to be similar to those of their neighbors. Most of them are currently well served by the tract builder and the remodeler who provides free design services.

Between these two demographic groups lies the upper middle class—the natural target market for design/build. These prospects will immediately see the value added by custom design, and they will be willing to pay for that added value. Thus, the clientele for design/builders of custom homes often are (a) the wealthy because they can afford a custom home or (b) the upper middle class because they value good design regardless of whether a name architect did it. For remodelers, design/build most frequently involves an upper middle-class client, and dollar value of the job tends to be lower than that of work designed by an outside architect.

Because of the lower dollar volume of remodeling projects and the intensive labor input for design, finding an architect who designs remodeling projects can be difficult in some geographic areas where architects have access to higher paying and less difficult jobs. Thus, in remodeling, design/build has opened up the affordability of good design to a larger segment of the population. However, design/build services usually are attractive to and purchased by the upper middle class (Figure 2-4).

Figure 2-4. Consumer Advantages from Direct Mail Piece

What is The McAdams Company Design-Build?

Design-Build simply means that our clients receive careful planning of their remodel or addition as well as quality construction.

Expert designers	Avoid "added on" look
Blueprinted drawings	Reduce jobsite errors
Detailed specifications	Your expectations met
Firm pricing	No surprises
Standard systems	Efficient construction
Experienced supervision	Excellent workmanship

Your project depends on good design and well-supervised construction.

For your remodeling or room addition call The McAdams Company at 822-6555.

Source: Reprinted with permission from Len McAdams, president, The McAdams Company, Kirkland, Washington.

Saves Time
If a consumer chooses to buy independent design services and then to buy independent construction services, the time spent from concept to completion usually will be longer than for the one-source shopping design/build provides. In design/build a number of design and construction phases can overlap. Estimating and specifying run concurrently with design. After working drawings, the work can move forward without waiting to find and qualify several bidders, receive the bids, decide the winner, and then wait in line for the winning bidder to fit the project into the construction schedule. With design/build the consumer is likely to be able to save 1 or 2 months over conventionally separated design and construction services.

Provides Go or No-Go Stages
With design/build the consumer can get a preliminary plan and estimate, decide that the project is feasible, and proceed or the consumer can decide that he/she does not want the project to proceed. Or just before working drawings are begun, the prospective customer can decide to put the project on hold and limit his/her expenditure. Contrast that ability with what happens when the consumer contracts for the designer's services independently. The consumer must buy design and then head for construction bidding before firm budget feedback is given. If the project is abandoned, it is usually after bids have been received and after full design payment has been made.

Projects are much less likely to be abandoned in design/build because budget and scope are frequently reconciled with constant feedback given to the client.

Cohesiveness Between Design and Construction
Just as the seamlessness between design and construction is enhanced in design/build for the professional, it also becomes an advantage for the client. Two independent professionals are not playing tug-of-war with the project. The same company that designed the job, also will construct it, and this company is more likely to keep the inevitable design decisions that arise during construction in harmony with the original intent.

Saves Money on Design
When the company designing a client's project knows that the design is for use by its production department, the level of expensive detailing of plans, the number of sections, and the specifications book can all be simplified to provide only the information that would not be understood by that company's production personnel. This simplification saves the consumer money on design.

Strong Working Relationship

Just as the design/builder benefits from a long early relationship with the client before the more difficult construction begins, so too does the client benefit from getting to know the company during design. Thus, the client can make a rational decision about whether to use this company for construction as well. The client also has no uncertainty about who to call, how the company will handle issues, nor about its attitude toward customer service (Figure 2-5).

Disadvantages for the Consumer

While many important benefits accrue to the design/build consumer, some disadvantages are inevitable. Design/builders must be ready to meet these objections in their sales presentations.

Potential Conflict of Interest

In the more traditional triumvirate of client, designer, and contractor, the designer and contractor usually review each other's

---

Figure 2-5. Design/Build Description from Packet Sent to Leads

JOHN CABLE Associates, Inc. is a licensed architectural and general construction firm that provides design and construction services. These services are combined into a design-build package or provided independently.

The design-build option is becoming increasingly popular because it has several advantages:

1. Design concepts are developed from the beginning that reflect a realistic understanding of construction costs and the budget guidance established by the client.
2. The design-build process delivers the completed project much faster than traditional design and construction methods. This time savings means cost savings.
3. The design-build package buys more for each dollar expended.
4. Construction is managed by an architect that is on the job daily. This ensures that the drawings are interpreted properly to implement the design intent.
5. The client's job has one point of accountability because the architect is the builder.

JOHN CABLE Associates, Inc. is unique in the way in which we provide the design/build service. We work to develop a design that meets the client's functional, aesthetic, and budget needs. The design also factors in our knowledge of the impact specific design decisions will have on real estate marketability and the economic return on the investment. After the preliminary design is approved, we prepare a planning cost estimate to assist the client in understanding the dollar consequences of various decisions that will be made in the preparation of complete construction drawings. Our experience in design and construction enables us to offer guidance in the selection of specific products, materials, and finishes that optimize the value received for the intended budget.

John Cable, President of JOHN CABLE Associates, Inc., is an architect and general contractor with extensive experience in the programming, site planning, design and construction of residential and commercial buildings. His projects include custom and speculative single-family, detached houses; estates; townhouses; patio houses; turnkey, military-family housing; and commercial buildings of a variety of types and sizes. Mr. Cable directed the Building Systems Research Program at the U.S. Department of Energy for 7 years, and he is internationally recognized as an expert in energy-efficient building design. In 1980 he was cited by *Engineering News-Record* as "one who served in the best interest of the building industry."

Source: Reprinted with permission from John Cable, AIA, president, John Cable Associates, Inc., Alexandria.

work and make changes as needed. The architect/designer can represent the owner's interests and is often paid to review the ongoing construction. This practice gives the client protection not normally available with design/build.

With a high-quality design/builder, the owner should have no concern about the lack of an independent third party. But if an unsophisticated consumer were to contract with an inexperienced or inept design/builder, the owner has no additional professional representation. No doubt under both scenarios, the client can be either well or poorly represented.

Lack of Competitive Construction Pricing
While many design/builders think that their approach provides the most cost-effective method of designing and building, the lack of competitive bidding creates the potential for an inflated price to the client. However, the design segment is more likely to be less expensive for the client when working in a design/build environment. Most remodelers and custom home builders simply try to cover actual costs with the design fee.

Architect design/builders tend to charge for design as a profit center but still are often less expensive than design-only services. The cost competitiveness of the construction segment is more difficult to assess. When the advantages of designing to client budget, functionality of design, careful choice of appropriate materials are considered, concern over lack of competitive pricing may be more a potential problem than an actual one. Given the final design, the design/builder is likely to be one of the high bidders if the project is bid out. In both remodeling and the custom homebuilding market, companies charging at or below their actual job costs abound. These firms lack knowledge of the cost of doing business, including overhead, and their net profit is poor. Thus, all established professional builders and remodelers will find competing on price hard, if not impossible.

Overhead can be called the cost of providing services. The more professional and in-depth those services are, the higher the overhead. Thus, design/build companies are not, by nature, shoestring operations. They have to look good, have great sales materials, brochures, stationery, do excellent marketing, and have the personnel to sell and complete this complex package. However, the economy built into the basic plan by a design/builder should more than overcome the higher markup charged by a design/build firm. Thus, a case can be readily made that the final job delivery cost is value-oriented and could quite possibly be less expensive than buying pieces of the job from independents.

Possible Lack of Insurance Coverage
If a project designer does not have errors-and-omission coverage, (which is more frequently the case of the design/builder), his/her clients are missing important coverage for building failure caused

by design malpractice. More importantly, these clients are likely to be unaware that they have such a gap in coverage.

Potential Low-Quality Design
A client can receive excellent design from either the independent architect or designer as well as the design/build firm. A client also could receive shoddy, low-quality design work from all those parties. Designs generated by design/build companies without trained design professionals on staff may be more work-a-day than inspired.

The design/builder also may be under pressure from the client's budget as well as under time pressure to move jobs into construction. However, a beautiful, functional, harmonious design is well within the grasp of most design/build firms.

Seeing the Client's Perspective

If design/builders are aware of the negatives and the positives inherent in this operating mode for their clients, they can be prepared to make the most of the advantages and to reduce the impact of the negatives as much as possible.

Through enthusiastic participation, the construction industry is making the design/build service mode more than a trend. The consumer as well has found many benefits from buying the entire package of design and construction services from one firm.

Notes

1. Linda W. Case, Part 6, "Production," *Remodelers Business Basics* (Washington, D.C.: National Association of Home Builders, 1989), pp. 166-94.
2. "Advantages," Chapter 6, "Marketing Customer Services," *Commercial Building: An Introduction for Home Builders* (Washington, D.C.: Home Builder Press, National Association of Home Builders, 1989), p. 120.

Marketing Design/Build Services

Marketing is a broad business function that encompasses every contact with potential clients. The design/builder's marketing mission is to make these contacts as numerous and as positive as possible with a particular focus on the true potential buyer of the service. Because day-to-day construction operations are public and because residential remodeling and custom building include constant inspection by a client, virtually no aspect of the design/builder's operation escapes public view.

Marketing ranges from advertising to trash management, from publicity to personnel behavior and competence, from participation in home shows to the appearance of the contract documents.

Design/build firms have a heavy marketing task. They must convince prospective buyers that they not only know how to build in a well-crafted fashion, but that they also design one-of-a-kind, beautiful and functional living spaces. The prospective buyer may ask, "Will this company understand my lifestyle?" or "Can they design a kitchen for me that's the most beautiful and advanced in my neighborhood?"

Design/build companies must project a stylish, well-considered marketing approach that assures the middle class, upper middle-class, or wealthy buyer that both design and construction services will be well delivered.

Targeting Marketing Efforts

Planning marketing is not difficult, but it is crucial. Targeting the prime job the company wants and the prime buyer of that job makes marketing much easier and less expensive. Some of the questions design/builders use to narrow the focus of their marketing programs appear in Figure 3-1. The brochure in Figure 3-2 provides an example of how one design/builder answered these questions.

> **Figure 3-1. Questions Design/Builders Use To Focus Their Marketing Programs**
>
> - What kind of job do I want? What kind of job do I do most profitably? What kind of job do I and my personnel most enjoy? The answers to these questions must address dollar volume, complexity, and type.
> - What kind of client do I want to attract? The answer here must harmonize with the answer to the first question.
> - How will I package my services? What "whistles and bells" can I offer that make my design/build services really stand out from all the others? Should contracts include interior design help in making selections? Should I leave the job broom clean or provide maid service at the end of the construction? The answers to these questions also must harmonize with one another.
> - How can I get others to refer my prime buyer? In other words how can I entice my prime buyer to call after hearing glowing testimonials from a third party? Prime buyers referred by a third party comprise the highest quality lead at the lowest price per lead.
> - How can I reach my prime buyer directly? Should I advertise, participate in home and mall shows, join the historic preservation committee?

Market Niche

Successful companies tend to be specialists. They attempt to precisely serve a need and a targeted client market by carefully dovetailing the services they provide with the needs of their clients. Design/build is a market niche. It involves packaging design and construction services primarily for the upper middle-class buyer. While the design/build concept can be purchased by every level buyer, it tends to appeal most strongly to the upper middle-class socioeconomic group. Therefore, each design/builder needs to assess the socioeconomic range of his/her intended buyer.

Although design/build is a specialty, it provides many subspecialties from which to choose. For instance, remodelers, custom builders, and architects may select commercial, retail, historic renovation, extremely large-scale projects, kitchens and baths, or energy efficiency. A design/builder also could specialize in a certain neighborhood. Choosing a niche (also known as positioning in the market) is one of the most important marketing decisions a design/builder can make.

While making the transition, a company may do all types of jobs for all types of clients. But once a design/builder sets the ultimate goal in job type and client profile, the company should direct its marketing toward that goal. Publicity, photos in brochures, written material, ads in magazines and newspapers should speak to the prime buyer and feature the prime job in order to attract those customers.

All company employees should (a) share the vision of the prime job and the buyer of that job, (b) work as a team to deliver the

Figure 3-2. Page from Marketing Brochure

Source: Reprinted with permission from Bob Lidsky, president, Hammer & Nail, Inc., Wyckoff, New Jersey.

> Our focus is on the entire space. ❖ Flowing from a total concept, we create a beautiful and unique design. ❖ This individualized method reflects both our aesthetic, artistic abilities and your needs, tastes and desires. ❖ Our approach is open to new possibilities and is fresh and varied. ❖ We are, however, grounded in the mechanical and technical fundamentals needed for a solid, on-budget, workable design.

> *A vaulted space is brought into scale with a cable-suspended light bridge. The walk-in pantry is concealed behind doors to the right of the refrigerator. Backsplash windows bring natural light to the verdi marble work surfaces while providing space for dish storage cabinets on both sides of the ceiling-height copper hood.*

Design: JAMES KERSHAW, CKD
Grand Prize Winner — NKBA Design Contest

company's promised services, (c) and move all members of the team in the same direction toward the same goal.

Company Image Once the company has targeted the prime buyer and the prime job, company image is the next marketing issue. Image must be compatible with market niche. The prospective client searching for a custom builder to construct a contemporary home may bypass the custom builder who is known for Williamsburg colonials. The remodeling client who desires a deck may not know that the remodeler who built the huge addition down the street also constructs decks.

All design/builders should answer these two questions about their firms' images:

- What is the company's image in the community?
- What image should the company project in letterhead, signage, brochures, marketing materials?

Community Image

All design/builders are projecting their image against an industry image. Designers and architects have a consistently positive industry image. They usually are seen as well trained, innovative, and service oriented. Home builders have a less dynamic industry image, and remodelers a spotty, but improving, industry image. These industry perceptions provide a backdrop against which any individual company's performance will be judged.

To assess a company's community image, the design/builder should be sure to regularly interview former clients, suppliers, subcontractors, and community acquaintances. Design/builders should ask for and listen for not just the positive pat on the back but also for the negative comment that will lead to improvements.

A potential buyer's image of the company is a digital readout composed of bits of gossip, seeing a company truck driver's driving behavior, meeting the carpenter at church, and talking to someone who bought a custom home or remodeling job from the company. Because of the nature of perceptions of community image, the design/builder must clean up and streamline virtually all company operations to present as many positive impressions of image as possible.

A positive image is a powerful force for a design/builder and must be jealously guarded. It can be affected by creating a high community profile. Many builders and remodelers are active in their local Chambers of Commerce, Better Business Bureaus, country clubs, Boy or Girl Scout troops, Lion's Club, and others. These organizations present innumerable opportunities to enhance a company's community reputation.

Company-Generated Image

Much of a company's community image can result from what that company purposefully projects. For a company with no marketing program, this lack of projection is a potentially dangerous omission. The company does not control its community image. It takes shape from uncontrolled, unguided perceptions in the community.

What are the components of this company-generated image program? In such a publicly viewed business, no aspect of a company can safely be ignored. The various aspects of company-generated image are discussed in the following paragraphs.

Company Name

In the building and remodeling industry, a company name that says nothing about what the company actually does is not unusual. Because of their names, such companies lose many opportunities. The buying public is literal minded, and when the sign outside the custom home says "Smith Associates," they are likely to think that is the real estate agent. Many companies have changed some part of their names to be sure that wherever their names are seen, the public understands what the firm does. In most cases, the important, familiar name identification is retained, and the following words are changed to reflect the actual business. For example, "Smith Associates" becomes "Smith Design and Remodeling." Every company needs to examine the appropriateness of its name and take action to improve the message if that is needed.

Company Office Open to the Public

The prospective clients who visit the design/builder's office consciously or unconsciously check both the design and the construction of that office and compare it to what they want in their homes. This tendency provides a heavy incentive for the design/builder to have a clean, neat, well-designed office with good craftsmanship (Figure 3-3). Many design/builders go much further than that, and turn their offices into one of their best selling tools. They frame and hang "good news" all over the walls—thank yous

Figures 3-3. Interior of Design/Build Office

Source: Courtesy of Tony Calvis, president, A.G. Calvis Construction Company, Phoenix, Arizona.

and complimentary letters from clients, awards, great photos, and association membership plaques. These design/builders do not have magazines in the customer waiting area, instead they have a presentation book or album of before-and-after photos of jobs well done.

Company Corporate Image Package

This fancy name for the design of all marketing material includes the logo, the company slogan, how the company name is written, what type is used, colors, and how they will appear, for example, on stationery, business cards, and brochures; in ads; on signs (Figure 3-4), vehicles, and uniforms; and on proposal presentation folders. A distinctive logo conveys the design/build firm's image and unifies the items on which it appears (Figure 3-5).

To have an entire image package consistently designed may cost

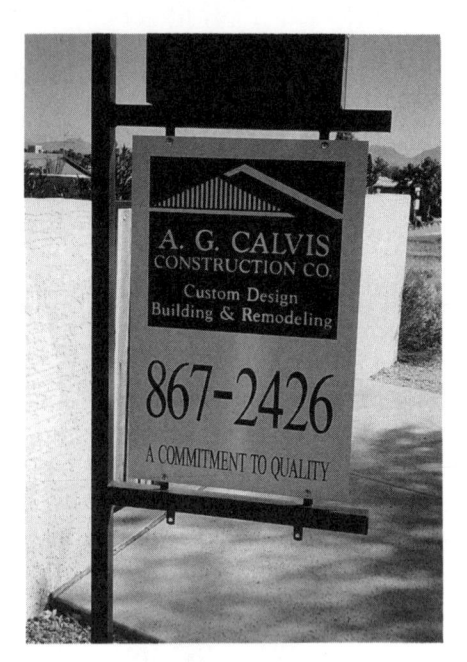

Figure 3-4. Office Sign

Figure 3-5. Logo

This unique logo commands a lot of attention whether it is on the company stationery, a portfolio, other printed material, signage, or in a company ad.

Source: Reprinted with permission from Jerome Quinn, president, SawHorse, Inc., General Contractors, Atlanta, Georgia.

$3,000 to $10,000 plus the costs of producing stationery, signage, and other materials. However, many design/builders barter for these designs or use in-house design talent to reduce the total outlay.

Corporate image is a critical aspect of marketing that is sometimes ignored by design/builders. The company owner may have come from a carpentry background, but if he/she is going to be successful in design/build, the company must have a truly outstanding image package. This one-time charge must be budgeted and purchased. Because the competition generally neglects image packaging, this one factor alone can help the design/builder outshine all other custom builders or remodelers in a particular market provided the firm backs up the image with high-quality service.

Personnel Friendliness, Competence, Courteousness, and Dress

Each company is the sum of its personnel. Today's design/builder must take extra care and train personnel so that customer care is uniform and predictable. Design/build is a service business not a product business. It is stressful on the client who, therefore, is not always polite and easy to work with. Design/builders have a tough task: to field cheerful competent workers despite poor labor markets, inadequate training, and a weakened work ethic.

Jobsite Appearance and Signage

Because prospective clients by the dozens ride back and forth past the jobsite on their way to work, to the grocery, to the dentist, and myriad other places, no design/builder can afford to operate without job signs. Job signs not only advertise the firm but market by association. This client has chosen this design/builder to work on this home in this neighborhood. That implicit testimonial or third-party endorsement provides powerful marketing. By the end of that job, neighbors will recognize the company sign and logo and be inclined to call the company for service if what they saw was positive (see signs in Figures 3-4, 9-5, and 10-1).

Human beings exhibit an endless fascination with construction progress, and jobsites are carefully watched. Therefore, personnel should always be appropriately dressed: no bare chests or halters should be allowed. They should park where they are least likely to offend the client and the neighbors and call for frequent collection of trash to avoid unsightly piles of it.

The experience of successful remodelers shows that jobsite marketing (Figure 3-6) is the second most fertile area for obtaining new leads after referrals.[1]

Many design/builders include in their marketing budgets regular programs of marketing to 50 to 200 neighbors of each jobsite. These programs can involve canvassing surrounding homes, hand-delivering brochures to these homes, or sending the owners a direct mail piece. These programs generate high-quality leads because

Figure 3-6. Postcard Sent to Jobsite Neighbors

Source: Reprinted with permission from Jerry Mesmer, Adams Studio, Washington, D.C., and Scott Watkins, president, Watkins Contracting, Inc., Builders, Remodelers, Designers, Arlington, Virginia.

each prospect can ask a neighbor how the company is doing on the job and perhaps even take a look at the project. Thus, the design/builder stimulates a referral with its marketing program. One Phoenix custom home builder has a brochure holder attached to the job signs. People take the material because he reports he must refill the holder regularly.

Vehicle Appearance and Signage

If a builder or a remodeler goes to the heavy expense of purchasing vehicles for company use, they should serve double duty by working as moving billboards with the company logo, name, phone number, and address. Magnetic signs should be avoided because they are more appropriate to the entry-level carpenter.

Design/builders should spend the necessary money for excellent, eye-catching signage for company vehicles. On the road in an urban area for 4.5 hours a day, a pickup truck's signage (Figure 3-7) could be seen by millions of people. No design/builder can afford to miss this excellent opportunity to promote company image.

Stationery Package

Most companies start with an off-the-shelf stock stationery from a national supplier. But ultimately companies want the stationery package—including business cards, letterhead, and envelopes—to express their own messages (Figure 3-8). Therefore they go to

Figure 3-7. Len McAdams and His Company Truck

Source: Reprinted with permission from Christopher of Kirkland, Kirkland, Washington.

Figure 3-8. Stationery Package

This distinctive stationery package stands out from the standard stationery packages available from off-the-shelf suppliers.

Source: Reprinted with permission from Dennis Huff, designer/supervisor, Homework Design/Build Remodelers, Visalia, California.

custom design. Stationery design would be part of developing the corporate image package and should be consistent in style, color, and type with all other company material.

The stationery packages of many established design/builders include a brochure about the company (Figure 3-9 and 3-10). This brochure ought to be consistent with all other marketing materials. The text should stress benefits to the buyer, and wherever possible, professional photos should emphasize the visual nature of the design/builder's work.

Publicity and Advertising
Publicity and advertising are two extremely powerful elements of company-generated image. All publicity and advertising either contributes to or detracts from the firm's image. Both must be

Marketing Design/Build Services   33

Figure 3-9. Inexpensive One-Color Brochure

The off-set fold makes this brochure distinctive.

Source: Reprinted with permission from Tom Gilday, president, Gilday Design • Remodeling, Silver Spring, Maryland.

Figure 3-10. Magazine-Style Brochure

The sale of advertising carried in this brochure to make it look more like a real magazine also pays for the printing of the brochure.

Source: Reprinted with permission from Jack Brock, CR, president, J. Duncan Brock Builder, Inc., Phoenix, Arizona.

carefully targeted to the firm's market niche to bring in the ideal customer. Because both generate leads so directly and powerfully, they are discussed later in this chapter under "Lead Generation."

Benefits of a Positive Image

While the work to produce a positive company image is never-ending, the rewards are widespread. Not only is the company able to do the kind of work it wants for the clients it prefers, but employees are proud to work for the firm, the bank is happy to have such an outstanding customer, subcontractors and suppliers want to be on the firm's winning team. Every corner of a design/builder's world is touched by the positive effects of an enhanced company image.

Lead Generation

The primary purpose of all marketing, image generation, and advertising is to produce high-quality leads. Leads are inquiries about a company's services from prospective buyers.

Lead Quality

Companies starting out in custom building and remodeling chase down and try to sell each and every lead with equal vigor. More established companies soon learn to qualify their leads and prioritize their handling. This practice allows the design/builder to invest greater sales energy into those leads most likely to turn into contracts and to handle those leads more promptly than low-quality leads as long as no prospective client is mishandled.

Companies in the enviable position of having more leads than they can service may refer low-quality leads to other design/builders and work only with those leads that best fit the company's predetermined buyer/job type profile.

Qualifying

Qualifying simply means identifying the clients most likely to buy from the company. Qualifying relates to close ratio. *Close ratio* is the average number of leads it takes for a company to sell one job. Thus, if a company sells 40 jobs from 160 leads, the close ratio is 1 out of 4. Qualifying helps a company identify leads that have a high close ratio and allows a company to reject leads with a poor potential close ratio. Identifying the company's market niche and target marketing to that niche helps to qualify the leads.

What makes a high-quality lead? Most design/builders agree the characteristics listed in Figure 3-11 are pluses. Not every one of those plus factors may be present in even a high-quality lead. To accurately evaluate each lead, design/builders should develop a lead form on easily identified, colored paper and collect consistent data on each caller.

Lead Quantity

At the beginning of business year, every design/builder should be able to assess how many leads will be needed to provide the volume

> **Figure 3-11. Characteristics of a High-Quality Lead**
>
> - Referral by a former client
> - Referral by a friend of the company, a supplier, or a subcontractor
> - Needs the services and/or products the company has identified as its niche
> - Appropriate geographic locale
> - Appropriate socioeconomic level
> - Sufficient home equity if borrowing is necessary
> - Time frame for project is within 1 year
> - Has not contacted other contractors
> - Has an appropriate budget range in mind
> - Does not have plans or blueprints yet

desired. Only simple information must be gathered:

- What is the company's average job size ("We built 10 houses last year for $2 million. Our average job size is $200,000.")
- What is the company's close ratio? ("For every 10 calls of inquiry from prospective clients, we sell 2 jobs. Our close ratio is 1 out of 5.")
- What volume does the company want to sell this year? ("Our projected volume this year is $3 million.")
- How many leads does the company need to sell that volume? ("To sell that $3 million, we need to sell 15 houses at $200,000. We will need to attract 5 x 15 or 75 leads to sell those 15 houses.")

The more qualified the leads attracted by the company, the fewer leads will be needed to sell the required work. Thus, if the company in the example above could improve lead quality and work with 4 people instead of 5 to sell 1 home, it would need only 60 leads instead of 75.

In their marketing programs, therefore, design/build companies must focus not only on lead quantity but on lead quality as well.

Marketing Indirectly to the Potential Client

The most qualified leads come indirectly to a company because they are referral leads, and they have built into them a third-party endorsement. Thus, they arrive virtually presold by a referring party. The referring conversation might have sounded like this: "We used Jones Design/Build for our custom home. I don't think they're the cheapest home builders in town, but we found we could trust them. They had great design ideas. We had a few snags as they built, but they always took care of them."

That free referral is worth hundreds of dollars of advertising that might lead a prospective client to the design/builder's door, yet the comparable advertising still does not give presold credibility to that design/builder. Thus, every marketing program should target referral-quality leads. The program must stimulate subs, suppliers, community leaders, real estate agents, and others in the community, as well as former clients to refer their friends and coworkers. Only if these indirect sources of leads fall short in producing adequate referrals, should the lower-quality, higher-cost leads of advertising be sought.

The most obvious source of high-quality, referral leads is former clients referring their friends, neighbors, and coworkers. Design/builders do not have to wait passively for referrals. They can actively increase them with a solid marketing approach.

Marketing to the Former Client
Without doubt former clients are the single, most important potential referrers in marketing design/build services. Marketing starts with a base of client satisfaction. The happy client tells 3 people about the company, but the dissatisfied, disgruntled customer greatly increases that number and tells 15 people.

With a base of satisfied clients the design/builder can market back to those clients in the two steps described in the following paragraphs.

Developing a Mailing List—If former clients number under 500 consider a copier label system from the office supply store, or freelance mailing list managers in every market will provide maintenance service for such a list. They will store the list, add names to and delete names from the list, and generate labels or envelopes on an as-needed basis. The computerized design/builder can generate envelopes or labels from the firm's own mail-management software. In addition to former clients, this mailing list should also contain the names of all potential referrers such as friends of the company, previous referrers, suppliers, bankers, accountants, and subcontractors.

Staying in Close and Constant Touch with Former Clients—Talk to them or mail something to them three or four times a year. This regular contact keeps their referrals coming in indefinitely and makes them part of the company team. They begin to have an emotional investment in the design/builder. Former clients also buy again. Recently a remodeler told of doing seven different jobs for the same family. A custom home builder in Texas built a married couple's home as well as homes for each of the spouses after they divorced and remarried. Staying in touch can take many forms:

- Send a thank you note for every referral. Just a quick paragraph that says "Thanks so much for sending Ken and Mabel Smith to us to discuss their new home. We couldn't keep building high-quality homes if it weren't for good friends like you!"
- Send a holiday card. Avoid the Christmas/New Year's holiday rush. Mail just does not get attention then. Consider Valentine's Day ("Roses are red, violets are blue, ...") or Halloween ("Remodeling is a tricky business, but it's a treat working with clients like you.") These hokey ideas prove eye-catching and memorable, and therefore, draw in high quality leads.

Figure 3-12. Newsletter Produced by Design/Build Remodeling Firm

Source: Reprinted with permission from Karen Galvin, marketing director, Anchor Design and Renovation, Inc., Newton, Massachusetts.

THE ANCHOR LINE

THE QUARTERLY PUBLICATION OF ANCHOR DESIGN & RENOVATION, INC./VOLUME 1, NO. 1/FALL 1989

The Anchor Line is a brand-new, quarterly publication from Anchor Design and Renovation, Inc. It's mission is to provide you with important information about home maintenance and renovation. The newsletter will also keep you abreast with new developments at Anchor, and introduce you to the members of our staff. We hope you enjoy the publication, and we encourage you to write or call us with any comments you may have about The Anchor Line.

Dramatic improvements to a kitchen can nearly pay for themselves when you sell your home.

Renovation Can Increase The Value Of Your Home

It's no secret that home renovation can be expensive. Depending on the scope of the project, a kitchen renovation can cost between $10,000 and $50,000; and a bathroom can cost $5,000 to $20,000. That may seem like a lot of money to spend, but you may be able to recoup these costs through the added resale value of a house. So the cost of the project isn't the only factor to consider when considering home renovation. You must also ask how your project will affect the resale value of your home. If you're planning to stay in your home for less than 7 years, the resale value of a project is a factor to consider.

Each year, Remodeling magazine, a leading-industry trade publication, surveys remodeling firms, appraisers and real estate agents to determine the price/value relationship of typical home renovation projects. The figures listed below are average resale values

---

- Consider a newsletter (Figure 3-12). Many businesses today are staying in touch with newsletters that have an informational message, give useful tips, and show interesting before-and-after photos of projects.
- Invitations to home shows and open houses. Any event that can be made social and for which an invitation can be generated can provide a chance to contact former clients. Thus, many custom building companies use an open house at a spec house as an opportunity to invite former clients to come by and visit.

When former clients visit, their bonds with the design/builder are strengthened, and often the former clients sell the prospective clients on working with the company. The design/builder who is going to be exhibiting at a home show can offer free tickets to former clients and invite them to stop by the booth.

If the design/builder does a good job and waits, referral leads will just happen passively. However, they can be greatly stimulated by an aggressive program of remarketing to former clients. With such a program, many successful remodelers and custom home builders receive up to 90 percent of their leads from referral.

Developing Friends of the Company
Networking is a major technique for developing new business throughout the business world. It is often overlooked and underutilized in remodeling and custom home construction. However, when a friend of the company, such as a local home inspector refers a new client, that inspector has supplied a referral-quality lead. Thus, referral leads can come from many sources, and the development of these additional sources should be a major marketing task for the company. The design/builder's marketing program could have the four major activities described below:

Breakfast/Lunch Program—Every month the design builder can take an influential community person to breakfast or lunch. The design/builder should pick the breakfast partner from potential referrers of the prime client and prime job. This person might be the banker, architect, accountant, economic development office employee, preservation society chairperson, real estate broker, or minister.

Organizations/Charities—Working with other community influencers on a common goal can be an excellent way to meet and greet potential clients. If the design/builder joins, he/she needs to be active, participate on an influential committee, and truly devote some time to the organization or cause.

Building Industry Associations—Every spec or tract builder eventually is asked to recommend a custom builder or architect. Remodelers who specialize in insurance restoration are asked to recommend a design/build remodeler. Design/builders should tap into the considerable amount of business that flows through industry channels.

High Community Profile—Many design/builders garner substantial work for their company through an active social life, by belonging to the right yacht or country club, fundraising for the right charity, or by holding a community office. All of these activities increase the referral of high-quality leads.

Positive Publicity
Publicity about a design/build company generates leads directly and powerfully. Much of what is read in newspapers and magazines is generated by the person or business about which it is written. A press release is a simple publicity generator. It should tell about some newsworthy happening such as a contest, receipt of a design award, promotion of an employee. Press releases about such events usually receive consistent, if frequently small, space. Before-and-after stories (which require photos from the design/builder) consistently garner media space (Figure 3-13). Some design/builders agree to do a regular column for a newspaper and that exposure can be bring in a steady stream of leads.

Figure 3-13. Reprint of Magazine Article

Source: Front cover, *Builder/Architect*, Arizona ed., Aug. 1989. Reprinted with permission from Robert Leveridge, owner, Sunshine Media, Inc., publisher of *Builder/Architect*, located in Phoenix, Arizona.

When a positive article appears about a remodeler or builder, the subject of that article appears to be a credible expert. Editorial space in a newsletter, newspaper or magazine is much more credible than purchased advertising space, and it is free.

Design/builders need to develop a program to garner local publicity. Often this program requires good professional photography and some ability to write. Sample story ideas might include—

- Beginning to plan your dream home
- How to pick a remodeler
- Before-and-after project story
- New trends in kitchen designs

The local "penny savers" (free neighborhood papers) are often eager for good photos and written material. If they target the specific neighborhood in which a builder or remodeler is interested in obtaining more work, they can be an excellent publicity medium.

Increasingly big city papers are devoting a section every week to the home, and that section should be a prime target for obtaining publicity. Design/builders should contact the editor or a writer whose name appears as a byline on stories and work to "sell" a story idea. Offer to provide professional photos and to obtain permission for publicity from the homeowners as well as to provide technical information for the article.

Obtaining publicity is only the first step. With permission from the copyright holder, such articles can be reprinted and used as handouts at home shows and be included in material given to prospective buyers. Such article reprints should carry the legend, "As featured in the Hometown Gazette," at the top or on the front cover. They should also be enlarged and framed for office walls as well as inserted in presentation books used in sales.

Publicity lends credibility to the design/builder's efforts: again it provides third-party endorsement.

Such indirect marketing is a much more effective lead generator than advertising because the quality of the lead is high and the cost is relatively low. The potential client comes to the design/builder by way of a third-party endorsement—a recommendation. Indirect marketing is a less predictable lead generator in terms of just how many leads will result from a particular effort. Unlike advertising, it is not a marketing "faucet" that can be turned on and off at short notice. Therefore indirect marketing should run year-round.

Marketing Directly to the Potential Client

Advertising can be looked at as directly placing a paid-for message to the potential buyer. It has the tremendous advantage of being relatively easy to start and stop as needed. The lead-generation effects of advertising usually become predictable in a given medium after a few uses. The disadvantage of the advertising-generated lead is that the person attracted has had no third party endorsement, so the close ratio is normally lower than for the referred lead.

Success in Advertising

The look, the message, the quality of all advertising adds or detracts from the positive image generated by the company. Successful advertising usually results from these three crucial factors:

- Successful advertising targets the desired client. Targeting often reduces the cost of advertising. The design/builder does not want or need to reach every person in the city. He/she wants to reach the potential buyer. That might be doctors and dentists, the upper middle class, or the elderly. Once the prime client has been identified, the design/builder needs to investigate how to reach that client.
- Successful advertising talks of the benefits. Many companies erroneously use institutional advertising instead of the action-oriented advertising they need. Institutional advertising just lets people know the company exists. The ad usually includes a photograph and the company name, address, and phone number.

It is not effective lead-gathering advertising. When potential buyers are reading the paper, they are not looking to buy a family room, they are reading the news. The design/builder's ad must reach out and grab them within a few seconds. To do that, it must clearly proclaim the benefits to the purchaser.
- Successful advertising urges the consumer to take action. Those newspaper readers are probably sitting in their easy chairs with their cups of morning coffee. What will it take to get them to clip the ad or to get up and call? Ads often offer a reprint, a gift, a coupon ("Yes, please send me the free pamphlet, *Designing Your Custom Home*.")

Advertising Media

As can be seen in Figure 3-14, lead generation methods can be evaluated on a number of criteria. Often high quality and low cost are associated, and those two characteristics are most frequently found together in the indirect lead producers. Low-to medium-quality leads and high cost often go together, and they are most often associated with advertising (Figure 3-15). However, when a design/builder assesses the quantity of leads possible from a given effort, that assessment may reveal that at least some ads are necessary for that design/builder's marketing program. The media most likely to be used by remodelers and custom home builders are discussed in the following paragraphs.

Figure 3-14. Criteria for Evaluating Lead-Generating Methods

- Quality of lead produced
- Cost
- Quantity of leads possible with that method
- Time required to set up and use that method
- Risk that the effort might fail (High cost and high risk are usually associated.)

Figure 3-15. Lead Producers

Indirect Lead Producers

Source	Quality	Cost	Quantity	Time	Risk
Referral programs	H	L	M	L	L
Networking	H	L	M	L-M	L
Jobsite	M-H	L-M	L-M	L-M	L
Signs	M	L	L	L	L
Canvassing	M	L-M	M	M	L
Direct mail	M	L-M	L-M	L-M	L
Publicity	H	L	L-M	M	L

Direct Lead Producers

Source	Quality	Cost	Quantity	Time	Risk
Advertising	M	M	M-H	L	M-H
Yellow Pages	L-M	M-H	M	L	M
Newspapers	M	M	M	L	L-M
Magazines	M	H	L	L	M-H
Radio	M	M	L-M	L	M
Television	M	H	M-H	L	H
Home shows	M	M	M-H	H	M

H = High   M = Medium   L = Low

Newspapers—This advertising medium is probably the most popular choice of design/builders (Figure 3-16). Newspapers make it easy and fast to place ads. Most communities offer a choice of newspapers—from the daily city paper to the weekly free neighborhood, "penny savers." Many design/build companies find that the small, free neighborhood papers are consistent lead generators. Lead quality and cost should be carefully assessed. A $50 average lead cost is a bargain; many companies pay $100 to $200 per lead.

Magazines—Magazines often target that all-important upper middle-class client and usually their photo reproduction is excellent (Figure 3-17 and 3-18). However, leads produced by magazine advertising can be stratospheric in cost. This advertising medium needs careful investigation.

Figure 3-16. Newspaper Ad

The headline in this ad tells the prospective client what kind of work the company does and its benefits to the consumer. The pictures in the ad draw the reader's eye down to the coupon and the coupon asks for action.

Source: Design and production by Kramer & Associates. Reprinted from Figure 123, Linda W. Case, *Marketing for Remodelers* (Washington, D.C.: National Association of Home Builders, 1987), p. 52.

Marketing Design/Build Services 43

Figure 3-17. Magazine Ad

Source: Reprinted with permission from Jeffrey Domowicz, president, Delmarva Design and Construction, Falls Church, Virginia.

Figure 3-18. Full-page Magazine Ad

Source: Reprinted with permission from Tom Gilday, president, Gilday Design • Remodeling, Silver Spring, Maryland.

Yellow Pages—Every business should have a listing in the *Yellow Pages* because the directories are so frequently used by the buyer to look up a phone number. Remodelers and custom home builders also use display ads (Figure 3-19), but they tend to generate low-quality leads. Many design/builders start with a large phone-directory ad and find they can reduce it over a few years to only a listing and not suffer from a lack of leads. Because of the high expense and inflexibility of this medium, design/builders should carefully investigate it before purchasing an ad larger than a listing. Precise statistics should be kept on how many leads are generated by the ad, the rate of conversion into jobs, and just how much each sale cost in advertising dollars. Only by keeping these simple data can the design/builder be objective about the worth of each ad medium. *Yellow Pages* ads can be the most expensive in terms of business generated for the dollars spent.

Figure 3-19. *Yellow Pages* **Ad**

Source: Reprinted with permission from Mark Beaton, vice president, Excel Design/Build, Capitola, California.

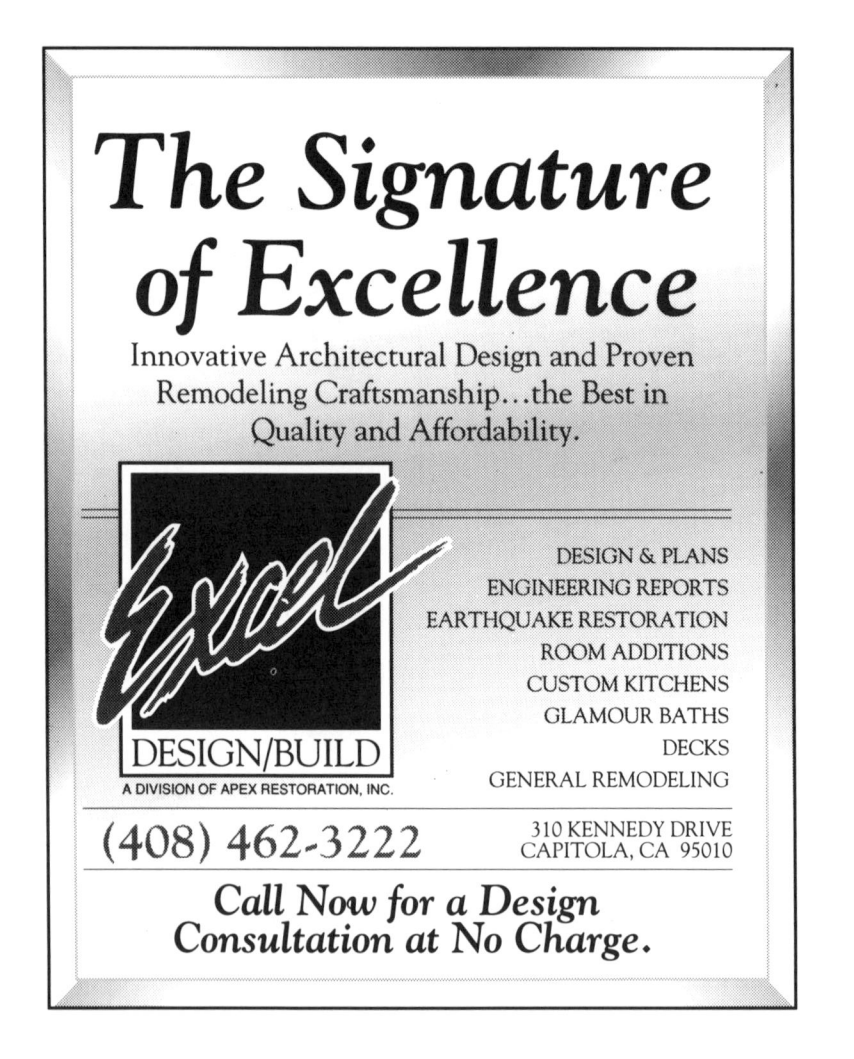

The Signature of Excellence

Innovative Architectural Design and Proven Remodeling Craftsmanship…the Best in Quality and Affordability.

Excel DESIGN/BUILD
A DIVISION OF APEX RESTORATION, INC.

DESIGN & PLANS
ENGINEERING REPORTS
EARTHQUAKE RESTORATION
ROOM ADDITIONS
CUSTOM KITCHENS
GLAMOUR BATHS
DECKS
GENERAL REMODELING

(408) 462-3222

310 KENNEDY DRIVE
CAPITOLA, CA 95010

Call Now for a Design Consultation at No Charge.

Radio—Radio is not widely used by either remodelers or custom home builders. If design/builders want to try radio spots, they need to look for a station with a demographic profile that matches the prime buyer to whom they want to sell. Testimonials from former clients can be a powerful approach for radio commercials. *Radio Commercials That Work for the Building Industry*, an audiocassette and checklist, provides some guidelines for using radio commercials.[2]

Home Shows—Home shows have sprouted in most areas, and they can be excellent lead generators or a waste of time depending on local conditions. Design/builders need to do some research, interview the owners of similar businesses who have marketed at home shows, assess the cost, and decide whether this avenue will work for their marketing programs.

Assessing an Advertising Medium

Because advertising of any kind is expensive, a thorough investigation should be made before spending any money. Tips for doing that appear in Figure 3-20.

Figure 3-20. Tips for Assessing an Advertising Medium

- Make sure the demographic group this medium targets matches the group the design/builder wants to target?
- Check the number of years this advertising opportunity has existed. If this is the first year, skip it until the track record can be checked the next year.
- Ask for names of similar businesses who have advertised and call and inquire about their results. Do they intend to keep advertising?
- Look at the quality of the existing ads. Can the design/builder meet or exceed that quality?
- Try to make a best-guess assessment of anticipated lead generation potential and cost.

Paying Commissions for Referrals

In some parts of the country, custom home builders engage in the relatively common practice of paying a real estate commission to a real estate agent who brings a custom home buyer to the builder. This commission varies from 3 to 6 percent of the home cost with the lower range more common. Custom home builders have mixed feelings about whether this marketing effort works. It does work well for some and not for others (see interviews in Chapter 9, "Design/Build for Custom Home Builders"). Obviously that kind of lead cost must be budgeted into the estimate and will raise the overall price of the custom home significantly. Despite this fact, however, this practice serves as a significant and successful marketing strategy for a number of custom home builders (Figure 3-21).

Figure 3-21. Real Estate Flyer

Source: Reprinted with permission from Rick Jennings, president, Rick Jennings Building and Development, Inc., Ormond Beach, Florida.

Rick Jennings

Award Winning Designs

Trust your clients remodeling to only the finest custom builder

- Quality craftsmanship
- Award winning designs
- Volusia's premier custom builder
- 1986 Builder of the Year

3% Sales Commission
(Based on contract price)

Free Consultation
Special Financing Arranged
Over 40 Yrs. Building Experience
State Certified - CGC-017050
Fully Licensed & Insured

5 Year Warranty Available
Call Bob Scott Today
673-0263 or 673-3051

"Your Design Team"
Bob Scott Judy Nichols
Rick Jennings Mark Pemberton

Marketing and Selling from a Spec Home

Both custom home builders and remodelers who do spec remodeling (a small, but growing group) agree that open houses and private tours of their homes currently on the market provide an excellent sales and marketing opportunity for capturing new work. The prospects who visit an open house usually are discontented with their present homes. If the open house does not meet their needs, they are candidates for a custom-designed home or a remodeling of their existing home.

The design/builder should consider a display set up in the spec house to sell services to the prospect who is not going to buy that existing house. The display could be similar to what would be used in a home show booth. Brochures or fliers should be available for distribution.

Planning a Marketing Program

Marketing has been overlooked so frequently in the custom home and remodeling markets that design/builders often can outshine their competitors with a well-designed, relatively inexpensive program. The key to developing an effective marketing program is planning. Only by careful budgeting and choice of expenditures in a one-year time frame can the company be assured of a consistent flow of leads of the required quality.

Some design/build companies do not plan their marketing. When leads are low, spot decisions as to how to advertise are made. When lead flow is good, no active lead generation effort is made. This start-stop approach leaves a company with few options but to rely on advertising because it is the only suitable lead generation "faucet." However, a planned approach is better because leads generated by advertising are expensive and lower in quality. The marketing planning tips in Figure 3-22 can make the design/builder's marketing more effective.

Figure 3-22. Marketing Planning Tips

- Assess lead generation needs. How many jobs will be needed? How many leads will it take to produce those sales?

- Develop budget line item. All design/builders need to budget marketing expenditures as a line item in the projected yearly budget. Many spend 1 to 4 percent of their anticipated volume. Because of the large dollar volume and small number of jobs, a custom home builder can often be in the 1 to 3 percent range. A remodeler will probably need 3 to 4 percent. Marketing must be funded on a steady basis because, when the money comes from a designated fund it proves less painful to spend the necessary money than when it has to be squeezed out of daily cash flow.

- Plan expenditures. Plan a year-round program that (a) attempts to obtain as many high-quality, referral leads as possible and (b) then uses advertising to obtain any additional leads that are needed. Review previous marketing efforts and keep the winners and drop the losers. Always include at least one innovative project in your marketing program.

- Develop a flow chart or schedule for when each task will need to be started. Part of scheduling will be to spread expenditures throughout the year on a practical basis.

- Keep simple lead generation statistics by source so the projections can be reviewed against what is actually happening. Reassess the company marketing plan quarterly to see if anticipated results are as good as projected. Make any adjustments needed.

Keeping Marketing Statistics

Simple data, faithfully kept, are all any design/builder needs to radically improve the efficiency of that firm's marketing program. The data design/builders need are described in the following paragraphs.

Lead Data—Design/builders need (a) to have all leads entered on a specific lead form, (b) to collect data on how each prospect came to call the company (lead source), and (c) whether that prospect ultimately buys from the company. In this way, not only the quantity of leads produced by a given source can be assessed, but also the quality of each lead source can be deduced from its close ratio.

Close Ratio—Every company needs to track its overall close ratio. If more than one person sells for the company, each salesperson's close ratio should be tracked as well.

Lead Cost and Sales Cost—Dividing the cost of a given marketing program (a home show, for instance) by the number of leads generated, provides a lead cost. This simple math allows the design/builder to assess lead cost from a radio campaign versus a home show booth. Average sales cost per client can be obtained by dividing the number of sales resulting from a particular marketing effort into the cost of that effort. For instance, the local phone directory ad may generate 30 leads for a cost of $900 or $30 each. Perhaps 5 sales result (a close ratio of 1 out of 6) for a per-sale cost of $180. In contrast fliers distributed around existing jobs may have produced 20 leads and cost $600. Those 20 leads resulted in 7 sales (a close ratio of 1 out of 3) for a per sale cost of $86.

Average Job Size
This simple piece of information is derived by dividing the company's volume in a given year by the number of jobs that volume represents. However, if this important information is tracked from year to year, it can show a remodeler how many jobs will be needed to produce a given volume.

Marketing as a Powerful Business Generator

Marketing can be inexpensive, creative, and a powerhouse for generating new business. It must be as well thought out as the design/builder's production systems. It needs to be budgeted and have someone who is enthusiastic and talented assigned to oversee it. Then the company must gather and monitor simple statistics as to how the program is performing in relation to goals.

Notes

1. *1987 Profile of the Remodeler and His Industry* (Washington, D.C.: National Association of Home Builders, 1987), p. 67.
2. Richard Elkman, *Radio Commercials That Work for the Building Industry*, (Washington, D.C.: National Association of Home Builders, 1988), 60-min. audiocassette and 8-pp. booklet.

4

Selling Design/Build Services

Once a prospective client has approached the company with an inquiry, how does the design/builder turn that prospect into a buyer? Companies need to develop a standardized method that works. They have a limited window of time during which they should sell the design phase with all the energy and professionalism they can muster. However, purchase of the design phase is also the qualifier of the serious buyer. If the prospect is not willing to buy the design phase, the free services the firm offers him/her must have a limit.

In choosing to be a design/build company, the custom home builder or remodeler also chooses to work with serious buyers. The design/builder knows that if the design phase sale can be made, the firm has a 80 to 90 percent chance of making the final construction sale.

The Design/Build Salesperson

Prospects who can afford design-build services range from the upper middle class to wealthy. The salesperson must be low key, well dressed, and able to communicate as an equal with the buyer. When a potential customer calls, he/she has a need, desire, or want. The salesperson's job is to define that need, desire, or want and present workable solutions that will excite the prospect. Therefore, consultative selling works best for design/build.

Selling design/build involves a consulting relationship at its best. It is not a hard-sell, one-solution, buy-it-now purchase. The salesperson must understand the prospect's lifestyle, socioeconomic level, and taste. This low-key selling of the design phase usually takes two to three visits. Both parties carefully assess how the other will fulfill his/her role, and both are ready to reject the commitment if all the necessary qualities are not present. Both parties also recognize the design phase as a first step and want to assure themselves that they want to continue all the way through construction together.

In custom homebuilding companies, this salesperson is quite likely to be the owner. In remodeling firms, the salesperson may be the owner or a commissioned, in-house salesperson.

Three functions are inherent in the selling of design/build services whether for a custom home or for a remodeling job: sales, design, and estimating. When the company is relatively small, these functions may all be done by one person. The design also can be done by an outside designer/architect as either an independent who contracts directly with the consumer or as the design/builder's subcontractor. In this case, sales and estimating normally are done by the design/build salesperson. An example of the various responsibilities of a design/build salesperson-designer appears in Figure 4-1. However, every design/build firm should develop its own job descriptions to suit its operations.

As the company grows, at least drafting is usually supplied to the salesperson, often in-house or on a free-lance basis. Large companies may also have a full-time estimator who supports the salesperson. The estimating position may also include responsibility for purchasing materials and supplies for production.

The plus in this multiperson sales capability is that each person's job is specialized, and each person can be first rate in a particular specialty—design, estimating, or sales. The minus is that accurate communication is required to make the system effective and efficient.

Selling such a big-ticket, complex package of products and services to today's consumer calls for a highly skilled and multitalented individual with excellent selling skills.

Figure 4-1. Example of Job Responsibilities and Performance Standards for a Salesperson-Designer

Overall Job Responsibilities

1. Perform the following sales functions per week:
   a. _____ Preliminary contacts
   b. _____ Survey and design
   c. _____ Presentations and closings
2. Be responsible for financial management of project.
3. Coordinate execution of projects with construction department
4. Develop sales skills through reading and exchanging ideas with colleagues
5. Possess expertise in light construction techniques and architectural design
6. Maintain sales tools

Performance Standards

Preliminary Contact

Initial Call

1. Be sure inquiry card is complete
2. Contact client within 2 days and arrange for interview within 2 weeks
3. Bring a list of past clients in customers area
4. Review neighborhood values
5. Bring list of professional colleagues
6. Know exact location of property

Initial Interview

1. Obtain information needed to fill out client profile report during conversation
2. Encourage prospects to describe living deficiencies and problems in their own words
3. Observe lot conditions and physically inspect home with prospect
4. Listen carefully to prospect's ideas
5. Briefly review customer's needs and ideas using photographs and the company's solutions to similar problems; note prospects comments
6. Suggest tentative solutions but stress need for detailed study
7. Qualify and establish budget
8. Arrange for presentation within 2 weeks
9. Determine survey area and set time for survey

Survey and Design

Survey

1. Complete prospect's profile form
2. Check zoning and building regulations
3. Complete survey in affected area per form and instruction sheets
4. Sketch rough floor plan of entire structure
5. Photograph elevations with particular attention to subject area
6. Prepare as-built plan

Design

1. Rough sketch design solution and review with president for approval
2. Prepare concept estimate
3. Review design solutions with clients
4. Listen intently to clients' comments
5. Obtain commitment to proceed with detailed plans and estimate

Presentation and Closing

1. Use supporting sales tools to reach final decision, including design building, photographs, and visits to other jobs and showrooms
2. Prepare final presentation for review by company president
3. Schedule estimating time
4. Prepare specifications, detailed plans, and contract
5. Arrange for presentation
6. Review plans and specifications item by item with prospect – reinforcing as necessary with supporting data
7. Obtain signatures
8. Establish financing

Financial Management

Estimating

1. Understand estimating system
2. Present complete project design to estimator
3. Be proficient in use of estimate
4. Review cost effectiveness of design with estimating department
5. Verify all estimate take-off totals

Figure 4-1. Example of Job Responsibilities and Performance Standards for a Salesperson-Designer (Continued)

Expertise in Light Construction

1. Be familiar with and know how to use the following reference books:
   - *Architectural Graphic Standards*
   - *AISC Manual of Steel Construction*
   - *Sweet's Light Construction File*
   - *National Environmental Systems Contractors Association Manual*
   - *Residential Lighting Consultant Course*
   - *Building Officials and Code Administrators International Code*
   - Zoning codes in all municipalities in which company operates
   - *National Electrical Code*
   - *Uniform System for Construction Specifications Data Filing and Accounting Costs*

2. Understand nomenclature of light construction industry and related trade (basic construction terms)

3. Understand technical application of the following:
   - Site layout and drainage
   - Footings
   - Foundations
   - Slabs
   - Masonry veneers
   - Fireplaces
   - Floor framing
   - Wall framing
   - Sheathing
   - Roof framing
   - Stairs
   - Exterior covering
     - Roofing
     - Siding
   - Exterior finish
     - Windows
     - Cornice and gable trim
     - Flashing and caulking
   - Thermal, vapor, and acoustic barriers
   - Interior finish
     - Walls and ceilings
     - Flooring
   - Doors
   - Trim and molding
   - Cabinet installation
   - Material handling
   - Heating and air-conditioning systems
     - Types of systems
     - Estimate heat loss and gain
     - Basic principles of design
   - Electrical
     - Code requirements
     - Recommended residential lighting requirements
     - Entrance equipment rating
     - Special circuits
   - Plumbing
     - Supply and waste systems
     - Recommended fixture layouts
     - Product knowledge
   - Architectural designs
     - Blueprint reading
     - Use of drafting tools
     - Skill to develop plan view, elevations, and cross sections from survey data
     - Skill to create marketable design solutions

Maintain Sales Tools

1. Present neat appearance
   - Hair groomed
   - Fingernails clean
   - Shoes polished
   - Clothes cleaned and pressed
   - Car well maintained

2. Maintain personal selling aids
   - Business cards
   - Brochure
   - Photographs and plans of past jobs
   - Current list of past customers alphabetically and by area
   - Letters of endorsement

3. Read the following magazines:
   - *Architectural Digest*
   - *Builder*
   - *Home*

Figure 4-1. Example of Job Responsibilities and Performance Standards for a Salesperson-Designer (Continued)

- *House and Garden*
- *Journal of Light Construction*
- *Professional Builder*
- *Remodeling*

4. Knowledge of referring customers as contacts
5. Maintain office reference materials
   - Product file
   - Sweet's Catalog
   - Design books
   - Practical guide to home landscaping
6. Be familiar with office procedures as they relate to customer contacts
   - Change orders
   - Billing forms
   - Building and occupancy permit applications and procedures
   - Subcontractors and suppliers
   - All forms used, such as:
     - Inquiry card
     - Contracts
     - Specifications
     - Information letter and tax form to customer
     - Sorry cards
     - Mechanics Notice of Intention
     - Mechanics Notice of Discharge
     - Jobbing contracts
7. Assist in maintaining showroom
   - Keep building clean
   - Record client visits
   - Keep files current
   - Project photographs
   - Project brochure
   - Leave showroom orderly for next sales presentation

Client

1. Review investment benefits of improvements and be prepared to compare
2. Understand and be able to explain financing available to clients
3. Explain billing procedures to clients
4. Be responsible for collection of all past-due balances

Coordinate Execution of Project with Construction Department

1. Fill out plan review and give plans to architect
2. Obtain sealed plans from architect as necessary
3. Check plans for code and contract compliance after receiving plans from architect
4. Upon receipt of building permit, check plans for additional requirements
5. Review contract changes with estimator
6. Deliver total package to office manager for processing and forwarding to production.
7. Assist in obtaining permits
8. Photograph existing conditions
9. Meet with construction superintendent and lead carpenter and review entire project
10. Meet with clients and project foreperson for initial project conference
11. Visit job weekly during construction
12. Respond promptly to design questions
13. Notify production of additional work
14. Expedite change orders for processing and obtain signatures and payment
15. Check at completion of job for total client satisfaction
16. Obtain endorsements from owners

Develop Sales Skills

1. Attend one course per year or the equivalent of 2 credit hours in any of the following subjects:
   - Construction
   - Appraising
   - Real estate
   - Interior design
   - Marketing
   - Management
   - Building inspector course
2. Keep diary of calls and contacts to evaluate effectiveness of sales effort

Source: Each design/build firm must develop its own job descriptions to suit its operations. This form is adapted from the Williams-Builder form in Figure 19-9, Linda W. Case, *Remodelers Business Basics* (Washington, D.C.: National Association of Home Builders, 1989), pp. 122-24.

The Art of Selling

Interviews with successful salespeople show they focus on listening, not talking. The most powerful way to sell is to listen carefully after asking open-ended, probing questions and then to return with carefully tailored solutions. If the prospects knew the solutions, they would carry them out themselves. They need the salesperson to solve their problems.

However, the prospects cannot always articulate their exact problems. The need for a large family room might well be a quest to get teenagers to spend more time at home. Building a new custom home together may signal a couple's renewed commitment to their marriage. If the salesperson can sense this underlying objective, the solution can be enhanced with additional benefits and features that will meet those underlying needs.

The couple seeking to strengthen their marriage may find a kitchen designed for two cooks or a design that focuses on the master bedroom and bath so compelling that the project sells more readily than it otherwise might.

The salesperson's careful probing and accurate listening leads directly to analysis and solution. In addition to a client's needs, design solutions for the remodeler must consider the client's budget, the existing home, site conditions, zoning requirements, the value of adjoining homes, neighborhood design considerations, and resale value. For the custom home builder, solutions must reflect client budget, lot selection, zoning requirements, composition of existing neighborhood, and local regulations.

This listening and analyzing is for naught if the salesperson cannot establish his/her trustworthiness and the company's credibility. Outstanding salespeople are not always extroverted, but they are always believable. Personal credibility comes from helpfulness, genuine interest, willingness to invest time in the project; a pleasant, uncontrolling personality; a track record of doing what is promised within the timeframe promised. The salesperson who is 15 minutes late for a sales call has established a barrier to selling. The estimate that is 1 week later than promised becomes a black mark against the company's record.

Company credibility comes from community image, the salesperson's ability to represent that company, as well as the quality of all sales supporting material (i.e., stationery, brochures, handouts, advertising, and related materials). Design/build salespeople should use presentation books or videos in their selling.

A presentation book (Figure 4-2) is a portfolio of work done by the company as well as information to educate the prospective client in buying design/build services. A well-produced video can replace a presentation book. Use of video presentation is finding favor with more and more companies today. The salesperson's presentation of photos and a short educational briefing should take no more than 5 to 10 minutes.

Figure 4-2. Developing a Presentation Book for Sales

Goals and Objectives
- To present the design/builder as a professional and to establish credibility.
- To educate the consumer in how to shop for a design/builder—to get the potential buyer to ask the right questions in case he/she is getting other bids or presentations.
- To standardize the company's sales presentation when more than one person is selling.

What To Include
Start with an attractive, professional looseleaf binder(s) with plastic covered pages. Check it every few months for wear and tear.
- ☐ A short company history—no more than three paragraphs—emphasizing the company's strong points.
- ☐ The license(s) required in your geographic area—explain its need to the consumer.
- ☐ Certificate of insurance showing required amounts of liability and Workers' Compensation insurance. Explain the importance of contractor insurance to the homeowner.
- ☐ If errors-and-omissions insurance is carried, explain its importance.
- ☐ Membership certificates for the trade associations to which you belong.
- ☐ Certificates for community association memberships such as the local chamber of commerce and better business bureau.
- ☐ Complimentary letters from customers and suppliers and thank you letters from community groups and charities.
- ☐ Before-and-after photos for remodeling jobs and photos of finished houses for custom building projects. Make the after photos larger than the before. After photos should be of furnished space.
- ☐ A checklist of important considerations in selecting a contractor. Checking all the boxes appropriate to your company gives the consumer something to use in evaluating the next contractor and weights the selection toward you.

Tips on Using
- Use the presentation book after the consumer has told the salesperson about his/her wants and needs. The salesperson can suggest that he/she tell the prospective buyer about the company, how it works, and show the prospect photos of similar projects.
- Keep the presentation book fairly thin and its presentation to 5 to 10 minutes. Avoid bulking it up with product information or samples. Put those in a separate book if necessary.
- All photos and paper should run in the same direction so the prospect does not need to turn the book to see the material.
- Insist that the presentation book be reviewed with each new prospect. If a customer does not want to bother, many companies instruct their salespeople to leave the meeting. Any salesperson who repeatedly refuses to use the presentation book should be dismissed.
- Consider role-playing practice sessions to train a new salesperson in how to introduce and use the book.
- One person should be responsible for updating the book(s) regularly.

The Process

Interviews with design/builders around the country show a strikingly similar sales and qualifying process. Each company has slight differences in its approach, but the similarities far outweigh any differences. Every firm needs to standardize its own process (Figure 4-3).

Figure 4-3. Questions To Ask When Standardizing the Lead-Qualifying Process

- How is the lead qualified and by whom?
- How many meetings are normal before signing a design contract?
- How many are allowable?
- What can be given to the prospective client at these early meetings (i.e., schematics, brochures, reprints)?
- Does the firm have a series of word-processed letters it uses to present a personal and professional appearance?
- Does the firm use a form photocopied on colored paper for recording standard information about the lead (Figure 4-4)?

The design/builder must stay in charge. He/she is the expert on the design/build system. When the system is well conceived and implemented, it will move prospective clients through the process effortlessly. Statistics on conversions to design contracts and the ultimate conversion to construction contracts will stay relatively consistent and predictable. Thus, thinking out this system carefully has long-term benefits.

Use of Letters

Many companies have produced a series of letters that blanket the prospect with information and create interest. They are simple to produce and can be easily personalized. If design/build firms are not yet on computer for word processing, they should be. However, a freelancer could put the company's letters on a computer and produce the documents as needed.

These letters should be friendly and professional and wherever possible should enclose an item pertinent to the job. This enclosure might be a brochure, a reprint, or a list of projects or references. A letter can be sent immediately after the lead is received (Figure 4-5). A second letter can follow the first sales meeting (Figure 4-6). Each additional meeting can have a short followup letter.

If clients have received a design agreement but have not yet committed to it, the design/builder should keep in touch both in writing and by phone. Many companies find that this contact ultimately can turn a number of undecided prospects into sales.

Figure 4-4. Example of Sales Lead Report

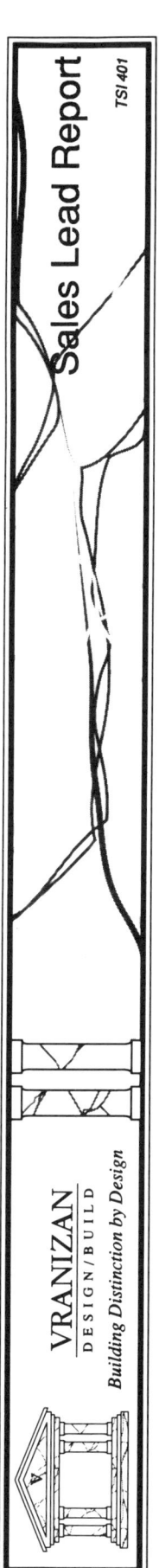

Sample: Reprinted with permission from Robert Vranizan, *president*, Vranizan Design/Build, San Francisco, California.

Figure 4-5. Example of Initial Letter Responding to Lead

Dear _____:

Thank you for your recent inquiry concerning kitchen remodeling. We are interested in helping you with your remodeling needs.

Our staff of professionals can help you to complete your project from start to finish. We can help you with the design, product selections, and construction. We are aware that most of the people who contact us have some idea of the scope of their projects, but usually they are in the beginning stages of the planning process. We are sending you a questionnaire that will help us evaluate your needs and allow us to be as prepared as possible for the initial consultation. Please take some time with all the decision-makers and fill out the questionnaire in a thoughtful way. Please return it to us in the enclosed envelope. We will call you in approximately a week to discuss your project.

I am also enclosing a list of some of our previous customers. Please feel free to call any or all of them to obtain a reference about our company.

I am eager to serve you in a personal way and provide you with the kind of service that would make your project enjoyable and successful.

Sample: Adapted with permission from a letter used by Todd P. Tomlinson, president, Tomlinson Builders, Inc., Damascus, Maryland.

Figure 4-6. Example of Second Letter to Lead

Dear _____:

I sincerely enjoyed meeting with you and discussing the project that you envision. I believe that the meeting was successful and positive. Your next step is to try to pin down the scope of the project in relation to your overall budget. I will be happy to meet with you again to refine the project and preliminary budget prior to beginning design services.

I look forward to meeting with you again.

Sample: Adapted with permission from a letter used by Thomas E. Mullen, president, Doubletree Construction Company, Inc. In the closing his name is followed by – Nationally Certified Remodeler, 1989 Regional "Contractor of the Year," 1989 National "Remodeling Designer of the Year"

Involving the Prospect

Many savvy design/builders assign "homework" to the client at each meeting. The client may commit to reviewing books and magazines on kitchen design ideas or visiting the top-quality plumbing showroom to begin pulling ideas together. This assignment is only partially done to simplify the selection process. Its main purpose is commit the prospect to the project and trigger his/her excitement about the project. It is one more way to raise enthusiasm about moving toward construction that is not at all burdensome to the design/builder.

"Yuppies" tend to be intense shoppers, and they know or quickly learn the difference, for instance, between brands of windows and other products that might be used in their design/build jobs. Knowing the prospective clients will want to heavily research product, the smart design/builder will get them started early.

Design/build should normally take two to three meetings to sell. If the prospect cannot commit to a design contract by that time, the company needs to move on. Sometimes design/builders make the mistake of trying to provide design during the free portion of the selling. While rough schematic ideas can be a tremendous and legitimate selling tool at this stage, going beyond that to refine design is almost always a mistake. It dilutes the value of the design contract. This line of demarcation between what is provided during the two or three free meetings and what is included under the design contract is crucial to the proper functioning of the design/build system.

The salesperson must keep the goals of the first meeting (Figure 4-7) in mind at this stage. He/she is selling only the design phase,

---

Figure 4-7. Goals of the First Sales Meeting

(Client on center stage)

- To establish the salesperson's credibility, trustworthiness, knowledge, and empathy
- To establish the company's credibility, track record, trustworthiness
- To give the client an understanding of how the company works, the stages through which the project's design and construction might progress, and how the company charges for those stages.
- To understand the client's needs, desires, and wants and to establish tentative priorities for them
- To establish preliminary project scope
- To establish a preliminary project budget and how the client intends to pay for it
- To assign fun "homework" for the client (i.e. visit the plumbing or the tile showroom)
- To set the appointment and agenda for the second meeting

not the total design/construction contract. However, selling the design contract will normally lead to selling the construction contract. The salesperson's job is greatly simplified when the focus is on a $3,000 plan rather than a $150,000 remodeling, or on a $7,000 set of house plans rather than a $400,000 custom home sale.

The First Meeting

For the remodeler, the first meeting will almost always be at the prospect's home. Changes to existing space cannot be meaningfully discussed without viewing and touring it. If the remodeler has a showroom, the salesperson may request that the prospect visit it to eliminate casual inquiries. After a relatively short discussion of the proposed project, the design/builder can then set up a meeting at the prospect's home. At the first meeting the design/builder might also give the prospect some suggestions for making the job go more smoothly (Figure 4-8).

The custom home builder can hold the first meeting at either the builder's office or the prospect's home. Most builders agree that if the look, size, and style of the office gives the builder credibility, at least one early meeting should be held there. However, the custom builder will gather considerable information from viewing the prospect's present home during one of the meetings. The prospect's lifestyle, house style, neighborhood, socioeconomic level, taste in home furnishings, and taste are quickly established.

Most design/builders agree that having a well-appointed office open to the public is a tremendous selling tool if it can be fit into the budget. Selling from the design/builder's own "turf" means increased control and the ability to have a multitude of samples at hand during discussions. Wall displays of awards, thank-you letters, and photos of beautiful projects provide credibility and can inspire clients to want their own remodeling job or custom-built home. In addition, in the office the client's television, telephone, and children cannot interrupt the meeting.

A tremendous amount of work has to be accomplished if the design/builder hopes to move the project into a design contract by the end of the second or third meeting. A first meeting should always start with friendly, open conversation. Both parties are trying to get to know one another, to assess competence, and to quickly learn enough about what the other needs to facilitate the process.

Scope

At this meeting the salesperson should view the client as on "center stage." The prospect should do the vast majority of the talking. All design-build buyers want to be listened to at this point. The salesperson's role is to ask probing, open-ended questions; listen; and absorb. Sometimes design/builders describe themselves as "sponges" at this stage. They work to absorb what the prospect says as well as all the visual cues. The design/builder must leave this meeting with enough information to generate one to three quick

Figure 4-8. Example of Homeowner Tips

TIPS ON MAKING YOUR REMODELING PROJECT EASIER

1. **START AT THE BEGINNING**: That means writing down how your home does not meet your current needs. Don't concern yourself with the physical design. That will come later. Just write down the problems you are trying to solve. Things like:

    * We entertain more than we used to and the house gets cramped at parties.
    * We're tired of going to the basement to do the laundry.
    * We want a bigger kitchen with an eating area.

    It is the solution to these problems that will insure that you will be happy with your project. Professionals can help with the actual design once you have stated your needs.

2. **PUT TOGETHER A BUDGET**: This may be the least fun but the most important part of the process. Everyone is different in how they go about doing this. But one suggestion is to find out what the better homes in your neighborhood are selling for. The difference between the current selling price for these homes and the price you paid for your house is a good indicator of how much you could prudently spend on the project and get your money back if you had to move within the next few years. This becomes less important if you plan to stay where you are for more than three or four years.

3. **FIND A CONTRACTOR WHO CAN DO MORE THAN BUILD**: Even the smallest remodeling project is complex and involves a great many people - city and county inspectors and officials, tradesman, craftsmen, vendors of all types. Not to mention a bewildering array of materials, colors and textures. Putting this altogether in a timely manner takes skill and management.

    Horror stories abound about contractors who took forever to finish a project because they were "good craftsmen" but "terrible managers". The choice does not have to be between the two. At SawHorse we pride ourselves on putting together a team of good craftsmen AND good managers to insure that your job will be done the way you want it - on time, within your budget, and with quality throughout.

4. **TAKE THE TIME TO ANSWER ALL THE QUESTIONS UP FRONT**: Once preliminary plans and budgets have been established there is often a tendency by all involved to rush into the construction phase. This can actually slow the process down. Take the time to specify and get firm delivery dates on all items BEFORE you begin construction wherever possible. That way you'll find out in advance if there is a long lead time on a particular item and a substitute can be incorporated into the design. At SawHorse, we take the time to plan and prepare so that the actual work can be done quickly.

5. **HAVE FUN WITH THE PROCESS**: The whole idea is to improve your living space and lifestyle. The way you go about it makes all the difference in the world. Know what you want; decide on a workable budget then stick to it; find a contractor who can manage the project and do quality work; take time up front to plan - and the rest will follow.

SawHorse

SAWHORSE, INC.
General Contractors
731 Highland Ave. NE
Atlanta, GA 30312
404/522-4542

Sample: Reprinted with permission from Jerome Quinn, president, SawHorse, Atlanta, Georgia.

design ideas/solutions for the next meeting. The sensitivity of these ideas will quickly show whether the design/builder is a good listener, not just for what the prospect says he/she wants, but also for what he/she really does want and need.

Many remodelers take photos of the existing home from many angles and perspectives to assist them with design and budgeting when they are working back at the office.

Budget

The client and the design/builder must establish a budget range for the project at this first meeting. The budget may change substantially as the client sees how features he/she wants raise costs. However, at this meeting the design/builder must make sure that the prospect is aware of a realistic cost range. Often when asked about budget, a prospect will say "That's why I am meeting with you." Then the design/builder presents some realistic budget ranges. The design/build salesperson should explain that the prospect will be making many selections and decisions and that each of these will either keep the project within budget or send it out of budget.

Budget should always be a range. For instance, if at this first meeting the design/builder believes the project is about an $80,000 addition, he/she should give a $70,000 to $95,000 range. A custom home range could well span $50,000 (for instance, $350,000 to $400,000). Even design/builders usually underestimate when asked to "ballpark" a figure. Intentionally lowballing or underestimating the project will keep the design/builder in the running for the job, but ultimately, it will mean losing the project when the estimate comes in out of range for the consumer.

Once a reasonable budget range is established, the salesperson should inquire about whether the prospective clients will need a loan and whether they have thought about what kind of financing they will obtain. Early inquiry about loan status is good homework for the client to start on. If the design/builder has financing sources, those names can be presented. They will also act as third-party endorsements when the prospect calls. Getting the prospect started on a search for funds may help to fast track the project later. A checklist helps the salesperson and the design/builder to be sure nothing is missed (Figure 4-9).

Selling the Company

At the same time the salesperson must use this meeting to establish his/her credibility and trustworthiness as well as that of the company. While listening to the prospect delineate his/her needs, the salesperson should suggest some ideas that clearly show the capability and understanding needed to give creative and well-designed solutions.

After the prospect has been carefully debriefed, the salesperson should give a 5- to 10-minute informational presentation on the company, a critical step. Established design/builders are virtually

> **Figure 4-9. Sample Checklist Used in Selling for the Design/Build Process**
>
> **Visualize Your Remodeling Project**
> ☐ Clip ideas and "looks" from magazines.
> ☐ Collect brochures.
> ☐ Visit model homes and shows.
> ☐ List your goals for the project.
> ☐ Make rough sketches.
>
> **Preliminary Design and Estimate**
> ☐ During initial meeting with contractor, measurements, goals, and budget target established.
> ☐ Preliminary plans, scope of work, and estimate are prepared.
> ☐ Follow-up meeting(s); plans, scope of work, and budget are presented; may involve more than one proposal to satisfy both goals and budget.
>
> **Plans and Specifications Finalized**
> ☐ Blueprints are produced.
> ☐ Subcontractors and suppliers give firm bids for their portion of the project to the contractor.
> ☐ Contractor develops critical path schedule, material take-offs, and pricing.
> ☐ Material prices, subcontractor bids, and labor costs are assembled on bid sheet. Contractors profit and overhead are added.
> ☐ Specification and construction agreements are prepared.
> ☐ All documents including bid sheet are presented to owners for signature.
>
> **Construction**
> ☐ Preconstruction meeting, familiarize the crew with the job.
> ☐ Site protection completed.
> ☐ Work starts.
> ☐ Hold numerous walkthroughs with owners during construction.
> ☐ Any change orders are agreed to in writing.
> ☐ Precompletion punchlist is developed by owners and contractors.
> ☐ Punchlist is completed by contractor prior to final payment.
>
> **Warranty**
> ☐ Design/builder provides 2-year limited warranty
> ☐ Warranty service provided by customer-service employee.
>
> *Sample:* Reprinted with permission from Jim Merrill, president, Merrill Home Remodeling, The JR Merrill Group, Renton, WA.

never the cheapest alternative for the prospect. Thus, they seldom win jobs based on price. Therefore they must proclaim and prove their value and quality. When the prospect is a referral, the third-party endorsement establishes some credibility and makes the design/builder's educational job much easier. However, when the lead has come through advertising, the design/builder has only a short time to educate the prospect and no third-party endorsement as a base.

This problem can be mitigated by providing references or by sending the prospect to a showroom where the showroom staff will congratulate the client on choosing the builder/remodeler with whom they are working. Many design/builders work hard at this first meeting to find a mutual friend or acquaintance who can provide this third-party endorsement. Use of a presentation book or video as discussed previously is a crucial tool for establishing credibility.

Explaining Design/Build

Many prospects may have heard of the design/build concept, but they may not understand it fully or accurately. The salesperson needs to explain how design/build works and the stages of the process. The salesperson must be especially careful to point out what is free in the process and where charges begin. Thus, if the prospect definitely does not want to work in a design/build system, the selling process can end immediately. Otherwise, the client leaves this meeting with a clear understanding of this chosen path.

Setting the Next Appointment

After obtaining information about the scope of the project, establishing a ballpark budget range, and selling the prospect and the company, the salesperson must decide whether the prospect is qualified to proceed with a design/build project built by the company. If not, the salesperson can politely tell the prospect that the project does not fit the company profile and hopefully provide the name of a remodeler or builder who is more suited to the prospect's work.

If the client does "pass" this initial qualification, the salesperson asks the client to complete an assignment for the next meeting such as cutting out pictures, tracking down the lot survey, or visiting the plumbing showroom. The second meeting time and date should be set at this first meeting. It is a commitment by both parties. An ideal time is 1 week later, but it should be set no further ahead than 2 weeks. On parting, the salesperson reminds the client of the second meeting and of what each party will bring to that meeting.

The prospects are enthusiastic at this stage, and that momentum should not be lost. If they are talking with any other contractors, those contractors may not be as well organized and prompt. By setting the second meeting and sticking to that commitment, the design/builder impresses the client with his/her organization and ability to deliver on promises.

The Second Meeting

The salesperson should reconfirm this meeting with the client a day or two before the scheduled date. The second meeting normally takes place either in the prospect's home or in the design/builder's office. The salesperson should be prepared to accomplish the goals for this meeting (Figure 4-10) with (a) a simple design phase contract (see Chapter 6, "Contracts for Design/Build Services"), (b) a ballpark estimate range, and (c) information on the scope on which that ballpark estimate is based.

The salesperson normally brings some quick sketches showing possible solutions to the second meeting, but these are not necessarily intended to be a final design resolution because that will be done during the design phase. The salesperson also reviews the budget in more depth to be sure that it seems adequate.

The salesperson takes center stage in this second meeting. His/her presentation should show beyond doubt that the prospective client's needs and wants were carefully assessed at the first meeting

> **Figure 4-10. Goals of the Second and Third Sales Meetings**
>
> (Salesperson on center stage)
>
> - To confirm the salesperson's credibility, trustworthiness, knowledge, and empathy
> - To confirm the company's credibility and ability to do the job effectively
> - To present two to three preliminary design schematics/sketches to the client to excite him/her about the project, to demonstrate the salesperson's ability to listen and understand the client's needs and wants
> - To sell the design/build concept and the company's ability to perform under those contracts
> - To close on the sale of the design phase
> - To assign additional "homework" to the client to keep the client committed to the project
> - To set the appointment and the agenda for the first design meeting

and that the company is able to fulfill them. Many companies provide simple schematic drawings at this meeting. If the company can generate them quickly and inexpensively, they are powerful selling tools (Figures 4-11 and 4-12). The company is trying to sell design, and these easily read drawings are worth a thousand or more spoken words. Often two or three designs are offered to show the range of possible options.

The company is not trying to design the exact home or remodeling job. That refinement takes place during the design phase. The design/builder firm is only trying to show that the company has talent, that it listens and is sensitive in response to the client, and that it will provide excellent service.

The salesperson will enthusiastically review the scope of the project and talk about an appropriate budget range. The salesperson should focus on the need for and value of the excellent design provided by his/her company.

Selling the Need for Design

Blueprints are needed by a number of parties for a number of practical reasons:

- They are the main resource for communication between the client and the design/builder on what is to be built.
- They communicate that design to the carpenter and other mechanics who will actually do the building.
- They are needed by various local authorities who will issue permits, check them with architectural easements, or allow changes to historic buildings.

66   Design/Build

Figure 4-11. Sample Schematic of Office Addition

Source: Reprinted with permission from Jack Brock, president, J. Duncan Brock Builder, Phoenix, Arizona.

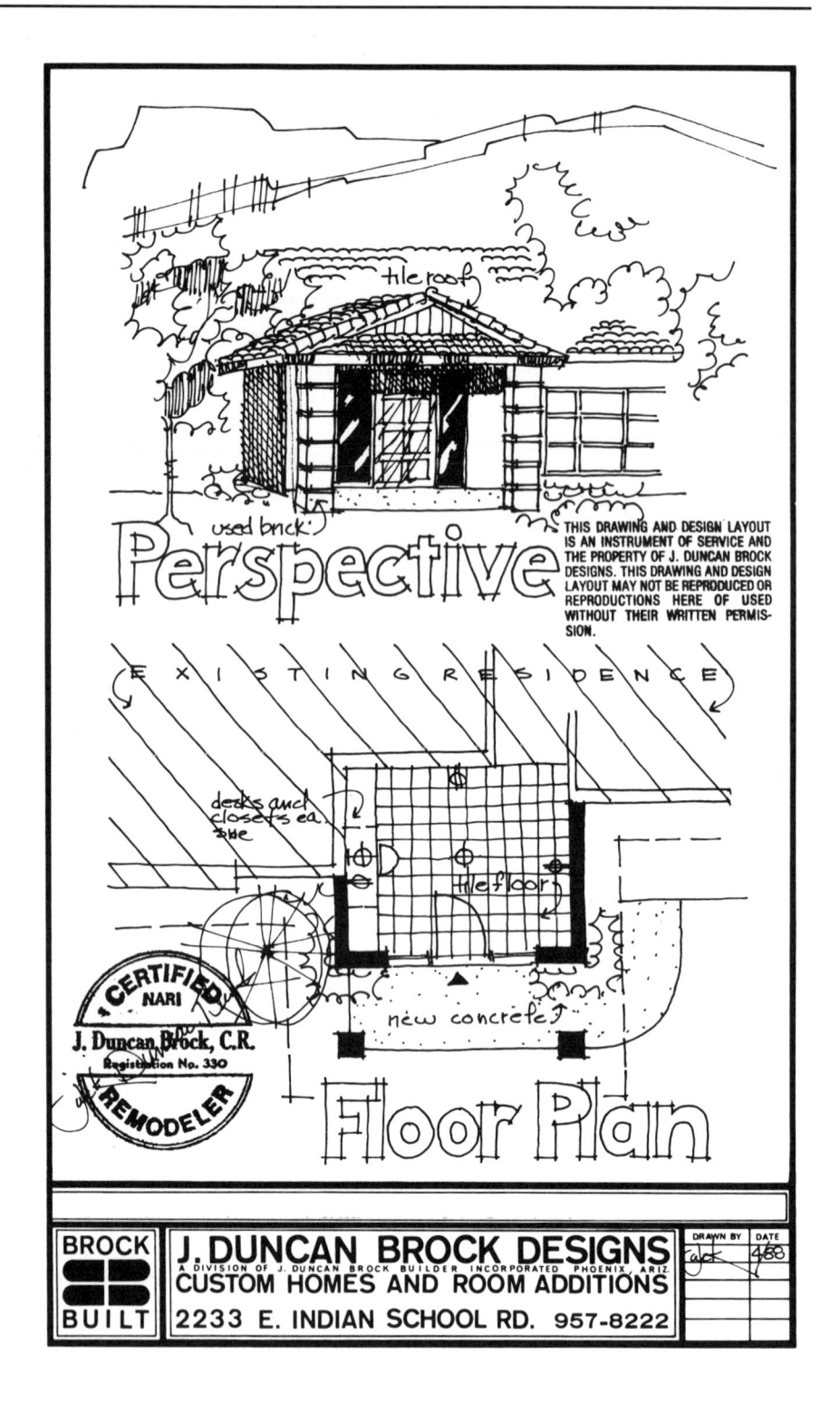

Selling Design/Build Services 67

Figure 4-12. Sample Schematic of House Addition

FIRST FLOOR PLAN
SECOND FLOOR PLAN

Source: Reprinted with permission from John Cable, AIA, president, John Cable Associates, Alexandria, Virginia.

In addition, design is critically important for a number of more abstract reasons:

- Good design adds value to homes.
- Good design makes living in a home more exciting and more comfortable.
- Design, carefully tailored to a client's taste and lifestyle, makes a one-of-a-kind, highly customized environment for that client.

The salesperson should review how the company's design/build process works, present and explain the design-phase contract, and then ask if the prospect has any questions. Many prospects want to think about the design contract overnight before they sign. Some prospects will hold that contract for a month or more before signing. If the prospect is not ready to sign at the second or third meeting, the company normally cuts off work with that client but stays in close touch. That can be done with calls, letters, sending an article or reprint so that the design/builder is always in front of the prospect's mind.

Those prospects who do sign a design contract proceed into the design phase of their individual projects. That phase is covered in Chapter 5, "The Design Phase." Selling—communicated through responsiveness, creativity, and careful budgeting—continues throughout the design phase. During this time, the client and the design/builder have an excellent opportunity to get to know one another and to work together.

Selling Construction Services
The next major sale is the big one—the construction of a custom home or remodeling. However, if the groundwork has been well laid and if the initial budget was adequate to cover the desired scope of work, this sale becomes simply a continuous move into construction. Upon completion of the working drawings, no surprises should occur. Design/builders who have been refining their design/build methods over a period of years, expect 80 to 90 percent of the clients who sign design contracts to sign construction contracts.

The most common major reason a client bids out a project after design is that the budget has been exceeded. The second major reason is that the client has not developed a strong working relationship with the design/builder.

In design/build each and every lost construction contract should be carefully analyzed to determine how the company might have saved that client. The design/builder may say, "It was the client's choices that put the project over budget, not mine!" However, most successful design builders refuse to draw an option that will put the project over budget unless the client agrees to change that budget. Thus, the design/builder works on the client's behalf as the guardian of the purse strings. This guardianship cannot be overstated.

Some design/builders keep a running sheet of options and their prices almost like a menu from which the client can choose. In this way, the base job stays within budget, and the client is able to see that it is his/her choices that push the job over budget.

In design/build the small dollar sale (design) is the big sale in terms of impact. The big dollar sale (construction) follows naturally if the principles of this method are carefully observed.

5

The Design Phase

When remodelers or custom home builders are setting up a design/build firm they must decide how they will handle the many facets of the design phase. Decisions will turn on the design/builder's volume, service philosophy, willingness to increase overhead, as well as legal direction. Questions that help to determine how to handle the design phase appear in Figure 5-1.

Figure 5-1. Questions To Help a Design/Builder Organize the Design Phase

- Will the design contract be broken down into a number of independently purchased parts or will it be one single purchase?
- What will the stages of design be? Will the final working drawings be made before or after signing the construction contract?
- Who will do the design? Will it be done in-house or out?
- How will charges for design be assessed? When will these charges be collected? Will the client be refunded any of this fee if he/she signs a construction contract?
- Who will own the design if a construction contract is not signed?
- How will estimating be coordinated with the design process?

None of these questions has only one correct answer. Successful design/builders mix a variety of approaches that add up to a smoothly running design phase.

The Design Contract

By signing a design contract, the remodeling or custom home prospect turns into a client. In doing so, he/she decides to trust the design/builder to match his/her needs and wants with the budget for a custom home or remodeling project. Thus, the client starts on the path through the process of designing a dream home or addition. But what will that path be?

Some successful design/builders use a single contract for the design phase to handle all aspects of the planning. Others use a two-stage design contract. (Examples of contracts for both design and construction will be presented in Chapter 6.) In a two-stage process, the first stage may be called the feasibility study or a preliminary agreement. It typically is quite inexpensive—perhaps $150 to $250.

During this feasibility study the design/builder goes into more depth in assessing zoning, in reviewing the budget and scope of the job, and perhaps in getting an engineering consultation. This feasibility study takes the initial free "ballpark" estimate deeper, so that when a full scale design is done, the builder seldom finds a problem that impedes the ability to construct.

Using a feasibility study allows the consumer to take a smaller, inexpensive introductory step into the design phase. This feasibility study might well be used in custom homebuilding to assess proposed lots. Many design/builders prefer to begin working with the client before any final lot choice is made, so they can advise the client about the site's impact on design and construction. At the same time the design/builder is assured of working with relatively serious buyers because they have paid for this feasibility review.

Design Phase Stages

Most design/builders retain some form of the traditional three stages of design (Figure 5-2) because they are logical and because they move the client from making the general choices (size and shape of space) through the ever more refined and specific choices (tile or wood floor for kitchen). These three stages are—

- Schematics or conceptuals
- Design development
- Working drawings

Remodelers normally also need some portion of the existing space drawn up as built. Having the as-built plans of the contiguous portion of their clients' existing homes allows remodelers to try many design ideas with accuracy regarding what currently exists. Often photographs or videos are taken of the existing interior and exterior to consult during planning.

Frequently some *schematics* or conceptuals—quick rough design ideas, often hand sketched—are produced during the selling phase. These sketches will go through further refinement in design. Remodelers use schematics (Figure 5-3) to help their clients choose the general design direction, so that they (the remodelers) can further refine the schematics in that direction. Any enhancement

Figure 5-2. Sample Design/Build Schedule

JOBS	Lead Received	Lead Qualified, Appt set	Appt 1	Appt 2	Appt 3	Appt 4	Appt 5	Appt 6	Design/Build Proposed	Design/Build Signed	Engineer Report Due	Site Checklist Done	Budget Defined	Preliminary Sketches	Engineer Report Done	Estimate Due	Estimate Done	Production Site Visit	Floor Plans To Be Ready	Contract Documents Done	Constr. Contract Signed	Pre-Construction Confer.	BUDGET	DESIGN $	EST. ARCHITECT $	EST. ENGINEER $	EST. GROSS PROFIT

Design/Build Schedule — TSI 402

Date: Salesman: Page ___ of ___   For:

The Signature of Excellence

Source: Reprinted with permission from Mark Beaton, vice president, Excel Design/Build, Capitola, California.

Figure 5-3. Sample Schematic of House Addition

Source: Reprinted with permission from Duncan Brock, president, J. Duncan Brock Builder, Inc., Phoenix, Arizona.

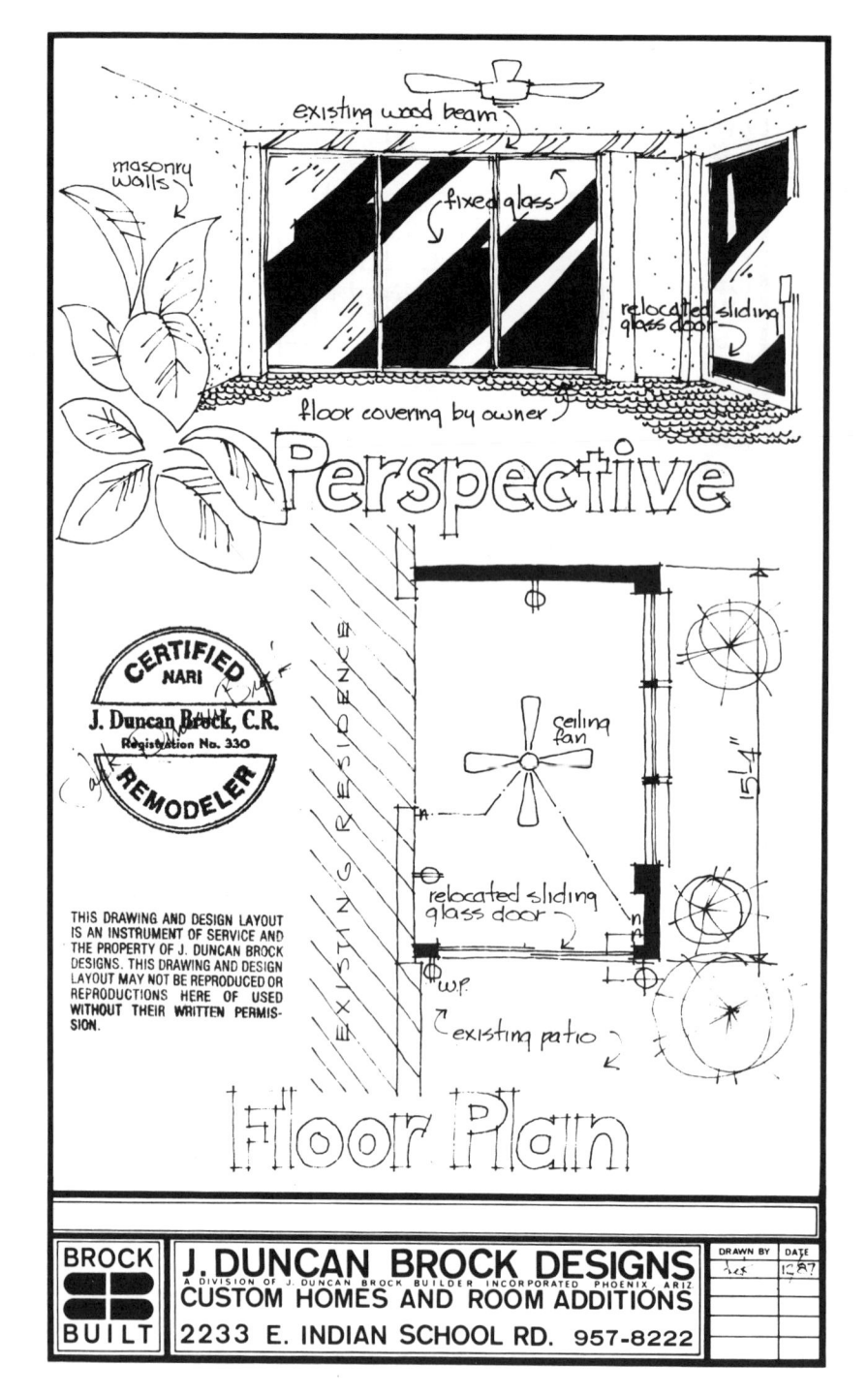

that increases the client's understanding of the conceptuals helps to sell the job because the client is more likely to buy a design he/she clearly understands. Thus, many designers include furniture and plants in the schematic to give the client a true sense of the space and to humanize the design.

Design development follows the general direction chosen by the client during conceptuals (Figure 5-4), and it fleshes out the choices in more detail. The focus continues to be helping the client to learn what he/she wants and translating those wants into an aesthetically balanced and beautiful solution.

In preparing *working drawings*, attention turns from communication with the client to communicating the design decisions to a number of other parties (Figure 5-5).

Some remodelers do the working drawings after a construction contract is signed. They work the design through with the client so all the client's needs for information about the job are answered by

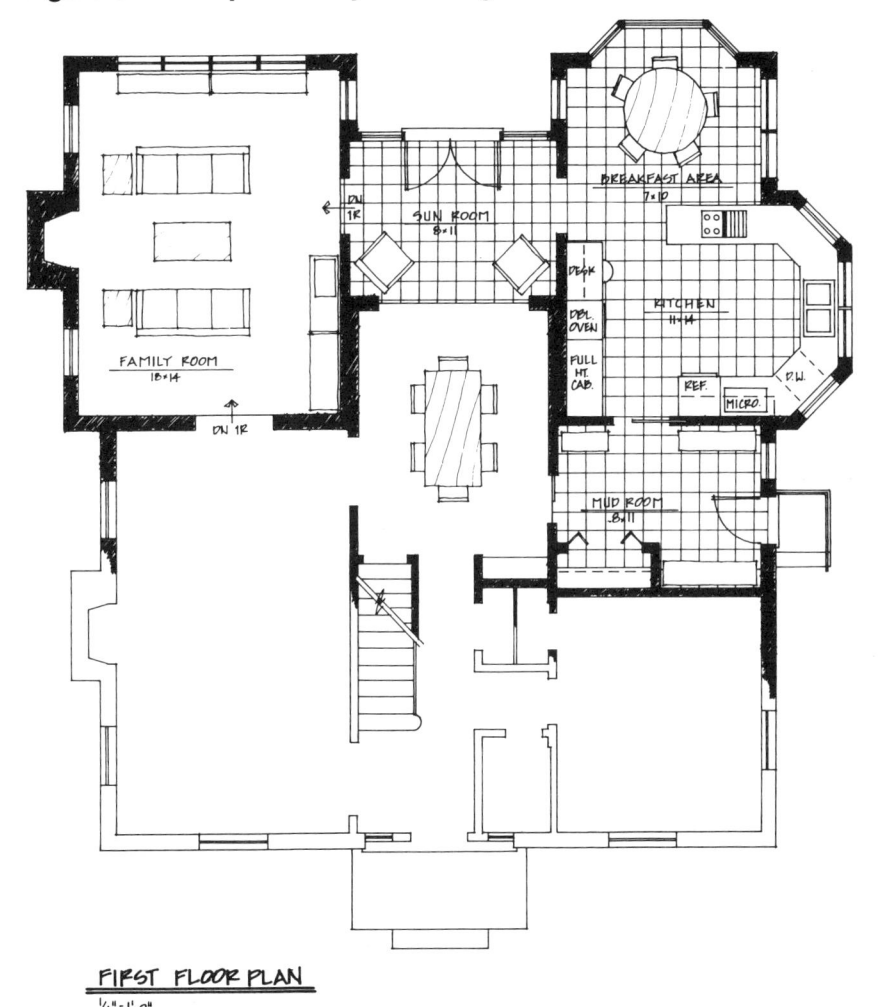

Figure 5-4. Sample Conceptual Design

Source: Reprinted with permission from John Cable, president, John Cable Associates, Inc., Alexandria, Virginia.

the plans, but they do not add the final how-to detailing and information needed for permitting and for the field personnel. This approach is typically taken by a firm that does not want to design for any other remodeler or builder to construct.

The client is told in the beginning discussions that the plans are for use only by the designing firm, and the design contract restates that restriction. In addition, the plans are clearly stamped to reinforce it. Thus, the company takes the plans through all the phases needed by the client. Only when the construction contract is signed are the final construction details added. If the client does not sign a construction contract with the firm, the remodeler has reduced the firm's liability from the construction of others. They also have reduced the designing costs incurred in the aborted design/build contract.

Figure 5-5. Elements Provided by the Working Drawings

- Detailing for the estimator so that an accurate final price can be given to the client
- Specifications needed by subcontractors for their accurate bidding
- Details and dimensions as to how the project will actually be built, particularly those details and dimensions needed by the mechanics to accomplish the project
- Information for the building code compliance personnel in order to obtain permits
- The foundation on which the design/builder-client contract will be based (Working drawings must contain the information needed to specify for the contract exactly what will be built and how and on what the final price is based. Most design/builders agree that making the working drawings as complete as possible is preferable to spelling out specifications in the contract.)

Designer Choices

The universe of design/build firms includes the small start-up business; the builder or remodeler who is shifting to design/build from using plans the owner already has obtained; as well as the large, highly professional design/build firm providing extensive in-house design services (Figure 5-6). This diversity has led to many different ways to provide the design option. The major decision is whether to employ design services within the company or to purchase those services on an as-needed basis from outside the design/build firm.

In-house Design

The advantages of providing design services in-house include full control of the process, the ability to continue selling the company to the client, obtaining production department input to assure that the design is buildable, and the ability to speed up or slow the design phase to meet production capacity. The disadvantage is that

Figure 5-6. Sample Rendering of Custom Home

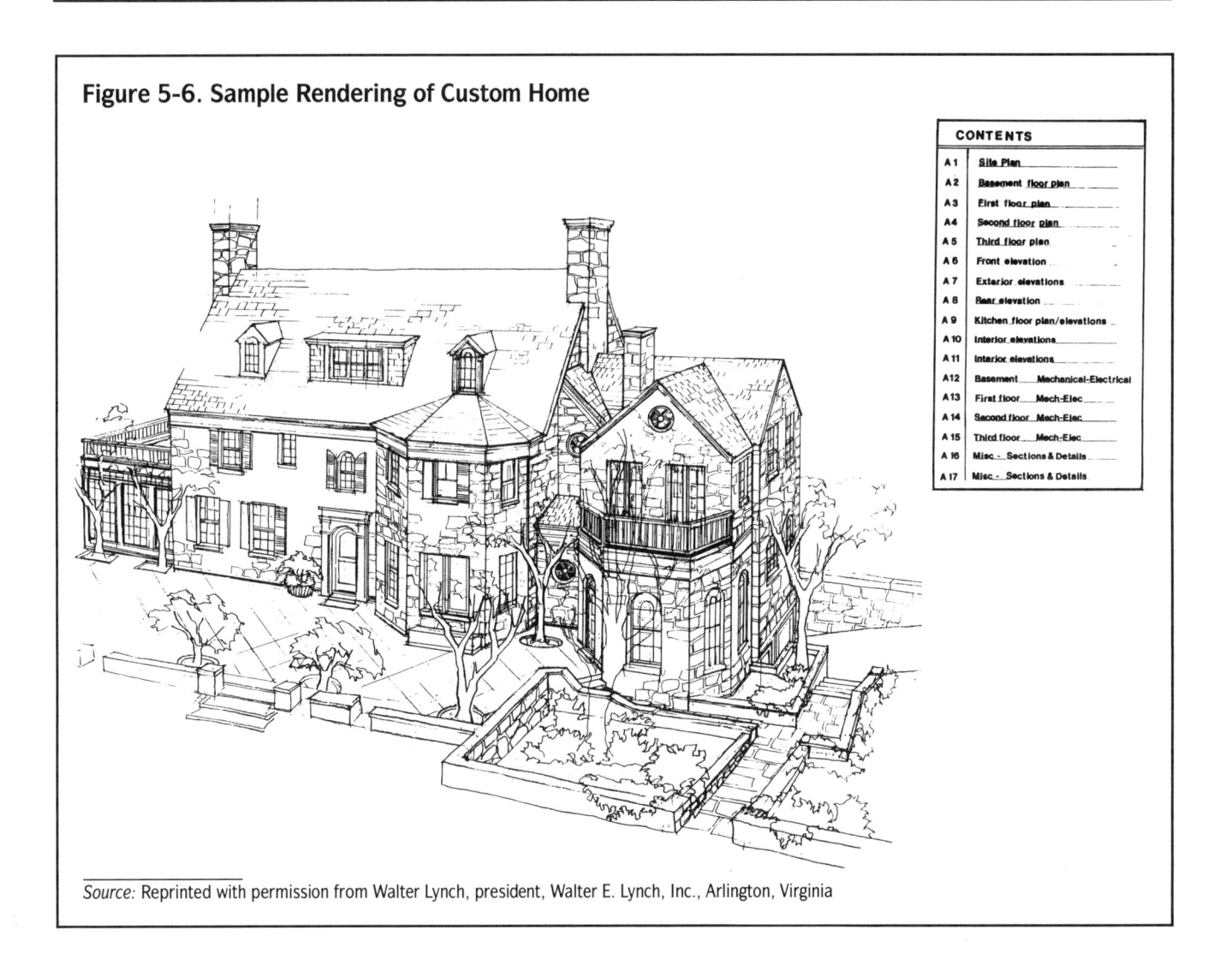

	CONTENTS
A1	Site Plan
A2	Basement floor plan
A3	First floor plan
A4	Second floor plan
A5	Third floor plan
A6	Front elevation
A7	Exterior elevations
A8	Rear elevation
A9	Kitchen floor plan/elevations
A10	Interior elevations
A11	Interior elevations
A12	Basement Mechanical-Electrical
A13	First floor Mech-Elec
A14	Second floor Mech-Elec
A15	Third floor Mech-Elec
A16	Misc - Sections & Details
A17	Misc - Sections & Details

Source: Reprinted with permission from Walter Lynch, president, Walter E. Lynch, Inc., Arlington, Virginia

overhead is increased and not all the available design service may be purchased by clients. In-house design departments also may not be able to provide the same wide range of design talents that can be utilized when design is subcontracted to outside designers.

Small-volume design/builders may add an in-house draftsperson to carry out design that is conceptualized by the company owner, who is the chief designer. Talented draftspeople can add substantially to the design ideas incorporated into a project. A draftsperson may be full or part time and could add estimating and purchasing duties to drafting if he/she is not fully occupied by design. When the company owner is the designer, time-management needs dictate that someone else do the time-consuming drafting work.

Large-volume firms may have a full-charge licensed architect or designer on staff who takes over the design function as soon as the design contract is signed. This designer works in tandem with the person who is estimating the project to keep the design on budget. The salesperson may stay in charge with the client or may provide only occasional input while the client works directly with the designer.

Many remodelers include sales, design, and estimating within the salesperson's job description. This combination creates a demanding and multiskilled job. Remodelers often hire former remodelers who previously performed all three tasks in their own companies to fill this salesperson's role. Custom homebuilders may perform all three roles, perhaps with some drafting backup.

Thus, a full range of professional design service is possible within the custom builder's or remodeler's organization. Designs can be as skilled and aesthetically pleasing as those done in outside design organizations.

Out-of-House Design

Every possible design service is available to the design/builder in the open market. However, the nature of design/build demands a close working relationship between the designer and builder or remodeler and developing that relationship can be more difficult with an independent, outside designer. The builder or remodeler who wants to develop such a design alliance needs to think through how the partnership will work and what each partner brings to the table.

Designer-Related Issues

Some of the designer-related issues to be considered are discussed in the following paragraphs.

Payment—Who will the client pay for design services? Does the client contract with and pay the design/builder? If so, all responsibility and accountability falls on the design/builder's shoulders. In the event of a design failure, the issue of liability falls on the design/builder. He/she is the prime contractor for the design and the actual designer is a subcontractor.

When design is subcontracted, the design/builder gains the advantage of control. It also reduces the danger of losing the client because the designer becomes part of the design/builder's team. For the client, this arrangement provides one-stop shopping and one-source accountability.

If the client contracts directly with an outside designer, the design/builder's input is often lost. Thus, to work this arrangement successfully, the builder or remodeler must have a clear agreement with the designer. This agreement should require the designer to dedicate him/herself to adhering to the budget; to work with the design/builder as part of a team, especially in controlling costs; and to encourage the referred client to return to the builder or remodeler for construction. The advantages of this arrangement are that—

- Design liability clearly rests with the designer
- Design capability can be matched to the client's needs.
- Design services can be offered without incurring costs by the remodeler or custom home builder.

The disadvantage is a loss of control over the design process and its connection with construction.

Working Arrangement—When the client is referred to an independent designer, will the client and designer work together or will a salesperson act as a go-between? Some design/builders feel strongly that they want each of their clients to work independently with the designer. Usually they develop alliances with architects or designers and recommend that the client contact the most appropriate designer. Or they may set up and attend the initial meeting with the designer. Under all circumstances the design/builder must stay in the designer-client loop to provide estimating services and to continue to soft sell construction to the client.

In some design/build companies that subcontract design, the actual designer is never seen by the client. The salesperson presents the drawings and returns to the designer to communicate the wishes of the client. If the design/builder views design as simply a practical step to construction, this operating style may work. For those design/builders who view designing as creative one-of-a-kind talent, putting these barriers between client and designer would not work effectively.

Alliances—Many remodelers and custom builders have lost potential projects by sending their clients to outside designers. If a true alliance has not been established up front, the designer may put the project out for bidding to a number of construction companies. A lot of business is based on networking and networking demands that referrals go back to the referrer of the business as a courtesy. No remodeler or custom builder should tolerate the loss of a client in such a manner.

In a few instances around the country, closer alliances are beginning to develop between remodelers or builders and architects or designers. In these more formal alliances, the two parties cooperate in a design/build partnership, but each also has other work that is not design/build. This win-win type of partnership is expected to increase in the future.

Charging for Design

Design/builders charge the client for design in different ways:

- Hourly rate
- Flat fixed fee for entire design or for each stage
- Square footage price—normally used only in custom home building

The design/build company picks the method (Figure 5-7) that is most suited to its operation and handles all design in the same manner.

Remodelers and custom home builders moving into design/build should assess how various purveyors of design in their locality normally charge. They should review both the total amount of the charge and at what stages those funds are collected.

Remodelers sometimes collect most if not all of the design fee up front. Custom home builders usually get a large initial deposit at the time the design contract is signed. Companies charging by the hour should ask for a retainer at the contract signing and then bill against that retainer.

A number of design/builders in both remodeling and custom homebuilding refund some or all of the design fee to the client who signs a construction contract with the firm. The final cost estimate of that project contains design costs as a line item so the design/builder is reimbursed for the costs. Being able to refund $1,500 to $5,000 against construction may be just the incentive to help the client decide to have that firm build the project.

If the final project estimate is higher than the original budget, the client is likely to want to end the relationship and demand the

---

Figure 5-7. Sample Schedule of Fees

Administration Fee (non-refundable):	$200.00

- Set up of files necessary to track the progress of your design project

Design Time:	$50.00/hr.

- Client meetings
- Preliminary sketches
- Design development
- Specification development

Research and Drafting Time:	$25.00/hr.

- "As-Builts" (Field measuring and drafting of existing conditions)
- Material research
- Construction cost estimating (Manual and computer generated)
- Drafting and blueprinting

Payment Schedule: Construction Contract
- 1/3 upon signing
- 5% upon completion
- Remainder to be divided by estimated weeks of construction (to be paid weekly)

Change Orders (Administration Fee):	$50.00 ea.

- Unsafe or unsound conditions found in the existing conditions during construction
- Client requested additions and/or subtractions to Construction Contract

Lightworks Construction, Inc. reserves the right to change these prices at any time without prior notice.

Note: Fees vary considerably from area to area and market to market. They also fluctuate because of changes in costs, interest rates, and other factors. These fees are presented in 1990 dollars.

Source: Reprinted with permission from David Johnston, president, Lightworks, Inc., Bethesda, Maryland.

return of the design fee. Often the design/builder thinks the client's decisions and selections put the cost over budget. However, the design/builder must understand that no matter who can be blamed, if a breakdown occurs it means a lost project. Therefore, the design/builder must safeguard the budget throughout the entire selling and design phases. Every design change that forces the project above budget needs to be brought to the client's attention so that the client can raise the budget or abandon the change.

Ownership of Design

Architects running design/build firms normally give their plans to their clients as part of the design phase. Builders and remodelers who have added design to their operation frequently keep the plans within their possession until the owner signs a construction contract. This restriction reduces the possibility of competitive bidding, but it is usually done for liability reasons. A company designing for in-house use can fit the level of detailing to the known skill and understanding of the field mechanics. Many sections can be omitted if they simply are the way the company always handles such a detail.

When they are designing for an unknown builder, design/builders must assume the worst and spell out every possible misunderstanding in detail. Since design/builders do not normally carry design liability insurance (errors and omissions), they must be extremely careful about who builds from their plans. Any structural failure on a project designed by them, no matter who the builder is, is likely to involve them in expensive finger-pointing and possible litigation.

Design/builders also should protect themselves by including in the design contract a clear statement that plans will be drawn for construction use only by their own firms and by stamping all plans similarly. Some design/builders while making clear their plans are for use only by their own companies do allow the clients to keep the plans in their possession during the design stage. Others do not. Each company must think out a rational system that is both user-friendly for the customer and yet protective of the company.

Estimating

One of the design/builder's great advantages over the independent designer is the ability to estimate as the project is designed. A large remodeling project or custom home may involve a number of estimates:

- The ballpark estimate before the design contract is sold
- The schematic estimate
- The design development estimate (Figure 5-8)
- The final fixed contract price

These estimates, which parallel the stages of the design phase, are normally ranges at the early stages. They get more and more precise as design decisions hone in on the final scope of the project. Even the final project estimate is likely to contain some allowances

> **Figure 5-8. Sample Short Planning Estimate**
>
> | | First Floor | Second Floor |
> |---|---|---|
> | General Requirements | $ 11,248.00 | |
> | Site Work | 3,982.00 | |
> | Foundation Systems | 10,125.00 | |
> | Structual Framing | 15,775.00 | $ 9,604.00 |
> | Exterior Envelope | 16,263.00 | 10,148.00 |
> | Interior Systems | 9,639.00 | 3,105.00 |
> | Interior Finishes | 16,412.00 | 8,230.00 |
> | Specialties | 16,146.00 | |
> | **TOTALS** | $ 99,590.00 | $31,087.00 |
> | **PROJECT TOTAL** | $130,677.00 | |
>
> *Note:* Cost estimates vary considerably from area to area and market to market. They fluctuate because of changes in material and labor costs, overhead costs, interest rates, and other factors. These costs are presented in 1990 dollars.
>
> *Source:* Reprinted with permission from John Cable, president, John Cable Associates, Inc., Alexandria, Virginia.

for still-to-be-chosen light fixtures, flooring selections, and tile choices.

One of the design builder's goals for the design phase is to arrive at finished design in line with the original budget or with a revised budget that the client clearly understands and has agreed to. The alternative is sticker shock on the client's part and the client's resultant attempt to salvage the project by bidding it out in hopes the scope can remain as drawn but at a lower price. In addition to missing the budget goal, the design/builder also has not achieved the goal of operating in the design/build mode.

Sometimes clients ask for a full breakdown of an estimate. Most remodelers and custom builders have found that giving those breakdowns starts a no-win process of the client picking apart the estimate. In general, clients are not willing to accept the overhead and profit needed by custom builders and remodelers and they must be "hidden" within the cost figures. Some design/builders, while refusing to do complete breakdowns, will breakout large scale figures such as "master bedroom option $12,000" in order to allow the client to choose from among options after seeing their general cost. More detailed breakdowns usually end in difficulty for the design/builder.

Another type of breakdown is often used by the design/builder to help alleviate the problem of the over-budget project. That breakdown is an options menu listing some of the items on the client's "wish list" that do not fit in the basic project but that the client might want to consider. For example the list might include "four skylights in kitchen" or "whirlpool tub in master bath in lieu of builder model" with appropriate prices.

Design Professionalism

Professionalism in design is best found in the quality of that design and in how it meets the client's needs and budget. However, the image of that professionalism is enhanced by high-quality drafting, lettering, and the overall appearance of the plans. No matter how good the design, much of its character is carried by these superficial elements of image. Design/builders need first and foremost to assure that design is excellent and then assure that the elements involved in its presentation also look excellent.

Design/builders should consider having a custom title block designed (Figure 5-9). Plans should be full-blueprint size and the drawing and lettering should be professional.

Figure 5-9. Sample Title Block

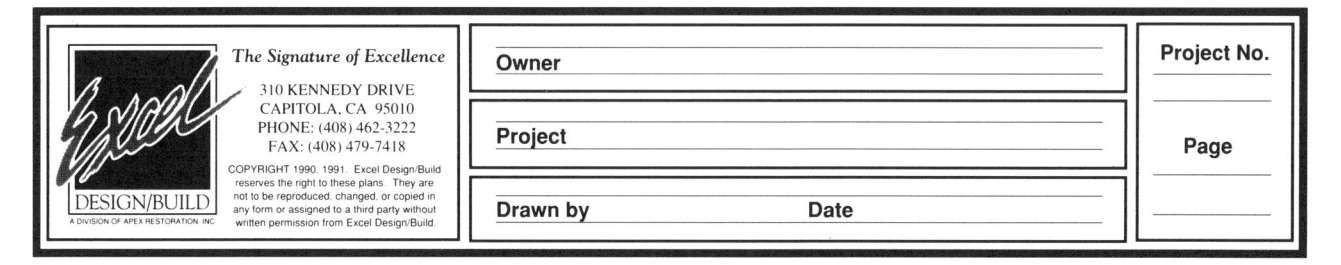

| Excel DESIGN/BUILD — A DIVISION OF APEX RESTORATION, INC | *The Signature of Excellence* 310 KENNEDY DRIVE CAPITOLA, CA 95010 PHONE: (408) 462-3222 FAX: (408) 479-7418 COPYRIGHT 1990, 1991. Excel Design/Build reserves the right to these plans. They are not to be reproduced, changed, or copied in any way or form or assigned to a third party without written permission from Excel Design/Build. | Owner _____ Project _____ Drawn by _____ Date _____ | Project No. _____ Page _____ |

Source: Reprinted with permission from Mark Beaton, vice president, Excel Design/Build, Capitola, California.

Use of CAD

A few design/builders have invested in full-scale computer-aided design (CAD) systems. Most of them are still quite expensive and need a dedicated operator—someone who works on the system much of the time. However, entry-level programs are also available. Full-scale CAD systems are not for 3 or 4 employees to share on an as-needed basis because people need considerable time and training to become facile with them. A design/build firm normally would have only one proficient operator because operating a full-scale CAD program is too complex to do on an as-needed basis like word processing.

CAD allows the design/builder to store frequently used plans, symbols, details or finish schedules and call them up for reuse at any time. CAD facilitates the reworking of a plan with a minimum of time and effort, much like a word processor allows for easy reworking of a letter in comparison with a typewriter. CAD can also be linked with an estimating database to cost out plans as they are drawn.

No doubt the current decade will see wide use of CAD in design/build. However, the systems must get cheaper, easier to use, and more versatile in order for most design/builders to purchase and use them. The ability to do quick designs and then to "walk" the client through the designed space will be a tremendous advantage to the professional design/builder. Clearly CAD separates a design/builder from the less professional remodeler and custom home builder.

The Design Phase Menu

The menu of how to run the design phase is full and varied. The concepts provide room for a small- medium-, or large-volume firm to customize operations to suit its size and locale. But the design/build firm absolutely must follow two bedrock principles for the firm to succeed: selling must continue during the design phase and the design/builder must protect the integrity of the client's budget as the design is being developed.

An Interview with Ken Foley

Ken Foley, a Vienna, Virginia, custom home builder and remodeler has invested in CAD. He has been in business 15 years, and his volume, between $1 and $2 million, tends to be split fairly evenly between remodeling and custom homes.

Foley is not a computer buff. In fact he says, "I had to be dragged kicking and screaming to computers. Our accounting software sat nearly 2 years before we got it running. But once I saw what it could do, I became very excited about computers." When he purchased his CAD system, he paid about $3,000 for the software and $500 for peripherals and a mouse. Foley decided not to purchase the plotter (the printer) and sends his discs to the blueprint company to be printed.

Foley reports that his plans are now more detailed because he can simply pull up a frequently used detail and put it on the current plan. The laboriousness of hand-drawing might keep a builder from this level of detail. CAD shines where recurring detail is used.

CAD does not save any time on the "the first generation of a plan," Foley reports, but "pulling a plan out of storage and reworking it is a tremendous savings," he says. Foley finds the greatest use of CAD in custom homes and much lesser applicability in remodeling because the work is so customized. He notes that his clients are impressed with the firm's use of CAD and with the professionalism of the resultant drawings.

Resources

McKendrick, John. *Implementing a CAD System*. Washington, D.C.: National Association of Home Builders, 1990. 18 pp.

Geoffroy, John, and Kay Rozea. *Selecting a CAD System*. Washington, D.C.: National Association of Home Builders, 1990. 18 pp.

Software Catalog for Home Builders, 1990 Edition. Washington, D.C.: National Association of Home Builders, 1989. 141 pp.

6

Contracts

A contract is an agreement between two or more parties for the doing (or not doing) of something specified. It is normally written and signed and is enforceable by law.

Design/build companies need to develop a sound contract that works for them and for their clients. Because laws vary from jurisdiction to jurisdiction, contracts in the building and remodeling industry are not standardized. Therefore, developing such a contract requires working with an attorney to design a custom document that suits the individual needs of the design/builder. Once it is developed, a contract should be viewed as a working document subject to revision annually or every 6 months.

Architects and their attorneys should investigate the standard American Institute of Architects (AIA) contracts because they have been carefully written with the architect in mind. They are widely used and inexpensive to purchase. However, remodelers and custom builders who are not architects will want to develop their own contracts with their attorneys.

For efficiency and cost effectiveness, contracts can be designed so that, while they cover the important differences inherent in each new project, a minimum of custom work is needed to prepare each contract. Most of the specifications for a job can and should be carried on the blueprints, which are then made part of the contract documents.

Contracts should also sell for the design/builder. The contract format should be well designed and attractive. It should reflect the company's professionalism. Often companies who use custom-designed stationery forget the contract is a critical selling document. Contracts should be printed on a letter-quality printer with the first page on company letterhead (Figure 6-1). To make

84 Design/Build

Figure 6-1. Sample Design Contract

VRANIZAN
DESIGN/BUILD
Building Distinction by Design

DESIGN AGREEMENT

This Agreement is between:

(name) _____ (address) _____

(phone) _____ _____

and **Vranizan Design/Build**, hereafter called Contractor.

Owner intends to remodel a _____ hereafter called Project, located at _____

Contractor will hold conferences with Owner and make or cause to be made necessary preliminary studies, working drawings, specifications, and large scale detail drawings as needed for construction. A cost estimate will also be provided.
Contractor and/or design personnel will meet with Owner(s) as follows:

1. One meeting to discuss, in a normal amount of time, except for preliminary drawings, not to exceed _____ hours.
2. One meeting for approval of the preliminary drawings with a normal amount of revision or design work not to exceed _____ hours.
3. One meeting for approval of the final drawings not to exceed _____ hours with additional design or correction work not to exceed _____ hours.

In return for the foregoing services, Owner shall pay Contractor the sum of $ _____ plus engineering fees (@ $135/hr), if required and/or energy calculations fees, if required. The payment schedule will be as follows:

_____

_____

If the scope of the work or the manner of it's execution is materially changed, or if the Owner requires Contractor to perform more than a normal amount of revision and re-design work, the compensation payable to Contractor shall be equitably adjusted with the following rates as minimum:
Designer / Contractor @ $ 75.00/hr
Drafting @ $ 50.00/hr
Engineer @ $ 135.00/hr

It is contemplated that, after the design phase is completed, Owner and Contractor will enter into a contract for the construction of the project. If, however, for any reason, Owner and Contractor do not contract for the construction of the project, Contractor shall deliver to Owner three sets of plans and specifications at no further charge to the Owner, provided Owner has paid Contractor all amounts due under this agreement. After delivery of the plans and specifications, neither party shall have any further obligation under this agreement.

Building Department submittal, fees, permits and/or corrections to plans are not a part of this design agreement, and must be covered under Owner's contract for construction of the project, or by others.

Contractor is not an architect, professional engineer, landscape architect, nor a building designer. However, Contractor may, at Contractor's discretion, employ the services of an architect, building designer, engineer, landscape architect, draftsman, or any or all of them, in the fulfillment of Contractor's obligations under this agreement.

It is the intention of the parties, Owner and Contractor, that the plans and specifications prepared hereunder are for the sole use of the Contractor in the construction of the project. Use of these plans and specifications by others releases and relieves the contractor from any liability for their use thereof.

All amounts paid to Contractor under this agreement will be excluded from the final contract price of the construction agreement that may arise between the Owner and Contractor for construction of the project.

_____   ___/___/___   _____
Contractor   date   Owner

Note: This contract is included in this book only as an example. Any contracts used by a design/builder must be created by the design/builder and an attorney versed in local construction law. Readers should not use any contract without first obtaining a legal review of it.
Source: Reprinted with permission from Robert Vranizan, president, Vranizan Design/Build, San Francisco, California.

the contract look more user-friendly, the design/builder could present it with a graphically pleasing cover or in a professional-looking binder (custom made or off-the-shelf with a custom label).

Contracts need to be in plain English that a prospective client can easily understand. The type size should be large and easily read. Clauses should be carefully worded and should make clear that the rights of both parties are being protected.

The development of a company's custom contract will involve some research. The design/builder should carefully think through needed clauses so that company policies are clear to the client. Then the design/builder needs the services of an attorney who specializes in construction law. The attorney should review the language, add any necessary clauses, and make sure that the contract conforms to local law. Under no circumstances should a contract be used without competent legal review, not even a borrowed or purchased contract.

The design/builder could potentially need three agreements or contracts: one for the feasibility study, another for the design phase, and a third for the construction phase. Most commonly design/builders work with two contracts, one to cover design and one for construction. However, some companies also combine the design and construction phases into one contract.

Design Contracts

The design contract normally covers the work to be performed during the design phase, frequently in a one-page document. This design contract should be in easily understood language and should contain the items listed in Figure 6-2:

Figures 6-1, 6-3, and 6-4 show three different types of design agreements. Any single contract may not contain all the clauses recommended by this book, but together these contracts illustrate the points made in Figure 6-2.

Construction Contract

The use of a written, custom-developed construction contract is essential. Contractors sometimes agree to use whatever contract the owner or the owner's attorney requests. That practice invites disaster. The design/builder will not know where he/she can get into trouble with that contract until it happens. Too frequently remodelers and builders do not even read those newly presented contracts carefully or obtain legal advice on them. If the contract is a standard one, such as an American Institute of Architects (AIA) contract, the design/builder may feel falsely protected. Any contract must be modified by an attorney to suit local laws and the design/builder's individual situation.

The only real way to know that a company is adequately protected by a construction contract, is to develop that contract with legal consultation, review it frequently, and revise it on an as-needed basis. No other solution exists at this time for the design/builder.

Figure 6-2. Elements To Be Included in a Design Contract

- The cost of design services—charged on an hourly basis, priced by the square foot, or totaled as a fixed charge for the entire service
- When that cost is to be paid—upon signing, in phases, or as billed
- The exact scope of the design to be provided plus a listing of how many floor plans, elevations, and perspectives that design will include
- The exact scope of the construction work ("a brick family room addition approximately 18x24' with masonry fireplace, wood floors, and 4 skylights")
- The budget range the design/builder has given the project ("a $300,000-350,000 custom home")
- Clear instruction as to who owns the plans and how they can be used ("Plans are for use only by Smith Construction")
- How outside services such as engineering will be handled and charged to the client, if needed
- Instruction regarding what will happen if the client changes the scope of the job, either by making the project (and the plans) more extensive or less extensive
- How the design fee will be handled if the client decides to buy construction from the firm (Some companies keep each phase payment entirely separate and do not rebate or credit the design fee against the construction cost. Other firms use the design cost as a deposit on construction. Still others may refund one-third or one-half of the design fee as a credit against a construction draw, preferably the final draw.)
- Notice of Right of Cancellation—if the sale of the design contract was discussed or made in a location other than the design/builder's place of business (Design/builders should consult an attorney for the precise instructions and notice that must be given according to federal law.)
- Any provisions required by state, federal, or local law

Figure 6-3. Sample Design and Drafting Agreement

Client _____

Street Address _____

City, State, Zip _____

Work Phone _____ Home Phone _____

Project: Room additions above existing low-pitch areas of house, totalling approximately 2,400 square feet.

Professional Services

Phase 1 – Having met with officials of the City of _____, we have left you a copy of the original hillside site plan of your residence that shows the outline of the planned house and ground elevations we will utilize in our drawings and eventual application for a building permit.

Phase 2 – This next phase in the preconstruction process of your project is (a) to perform field measurements to correct the original house layout portion of the site plan and (b) to determine the interior basic room layouts of the areas that we will be affecting by the room additions.

Phase 3 – This phase will include preparation of informal, to-scale layouts of the new master suite (with entry stairs from the existing master suite, which we are to remodel to become a library with limited bath); the three-bedroom, two-bath addition at the opposite end; and conversion of the existing downstairs rooms to include the new stairway, exercise room, and the guest room, as well as the connecting hallway/gallery above the existing patio. Included in this phase are meetings by phone or in person regarding project design, redesign, or changes and meetings with engineers or building inspectors relating to the design of your project.

Phase 4 – Provide working drawings from the approved preliminary designs that show you specific project information. Working drawings also serve for contractor estimating, building permit application, and for construction.

Engineering will be required because of the scope of your project. Prior to hiring the engineer we will advise you as to cost of those services, and we will bill you for their charges.

Professional Fees

Phases 1 and 2 – Secure site plan, verify existing measurements of exterior construction, and field measure affected interior areas, $500.00

Phases 3 and 4 – In-scale preliminary design work and working drawings, $1.00 per square foot of area requiring structural considerations, approximately $2,400.00.

Terms of Payment

Phases 1 and 2 will require: a payment of $500.00 on the day that we begin phase 2.

Phases 3 and 4 will require:

1/3 of the estimated fee prior to preliminary design;

1/3 of the estimated fee upon your approval of the preliminary design and prior to our beginning of working drawings;

the balance of our fee, engineering fees, and printing costs are due upon delivery to you of completed working drawings for your project.

Please note that changes following approval of preliminary drawings and commencement of working drawings generally require changes throughout the working drawings, and will be billed at the rate of $40.00 per hour. Printing and other reimbursables shall be billed at 1.15 times our cost.

If you choose to terminate our Agreement during the various phases of preconstruction, we will bill or credit you based upon our actual involvement to that date.

_____ Date _____
President

Authorized by: _____ Date _____

Note: This contract is included in this book only as an example. Any contracts used by a design/builder must be created by the design/builder and an attorney versed in local construction law. Readers should not use any contract without first obtaining a legal review of it.

Source: Adapted with permission from Tom Mullen, CR, president, Doubletree Construction Company, Inc., Scottsdale, Arizona.

88 *Design/Build*

Figure 6-4. Sample Design Contract

Client Name _____

Address _____

_____

_____

Home Phone _____ Work Phone _____

The McAdams Company, referred to as Designer in this proposal, will provide the following plans and/or design services for the Client named above.

Descriptions

_____ Floor plan(s) of existing spaces   _____

_____ Floor plan(s) of new or revised spaces   _____

_____ Exterior elevation(s)   _____

_____ Interior elevation(s)   _____

_____ Electrical plan(s)   _____

Other plans or special details to be included are as follows:

_____

_____

Unless otherwise noted all plans will be drawn @ 1/4" scale and one blueprinted set provided to client for permanent record. Plans are prepared to meet prevailing building codes when ued in The McAdams Company standard procedures. Anyone using thee drawings should field verify any and all conditions, dimensions, and conformity with codes and the adequacy of the drawings.

There are no other agreements between the parties except those expressly stated herein. Any amendments to this agreement shall be in writing signed by both parties. In the event of a dispute between the parties, any claim for damages against the Designer arising from, or related to, the services provided hereunder, shall be limited to the amount of money received by Designer pursuant to this agreement.

The Designer proposes to furnish design services as specified above for the sum of _____ dollars $ _____

Payment to be made as follows: _____

Date _____ Authorized signature _____

The above listed prices, specifications, and conditions are satisfactfory and are hereby accepted. You are authorized to do the work as specified. Payment will be made as outlined above.

Date of acceptance _____ Signature _____

Signature _____

Note: This contract is included in this book only as an example. Any contracts used by a design/builder must be created by the design/builder and an attorney versed in local construction law. Readers should not use any contract without first obtaining a legal review of it.

Source: Reprinted with permission from Len McAdams, president, The McAdams Company, Kirkland, Washington.

Design/builders could easily focus on a contract as a means of protecting themselves from serious legal consequences, but first and foremost, a contract is a sincere effort to communicate each party's responsibilities to the client. The contract should focus on how the company expects to operate, what services and products it will deliver to the client, and what it will not deliver. A contract should make clear the client's responsibilities in the relationship.

If some aspect of a contract is ambiguous or unclear, that ambiguity or lack of clarity will be held against the writer of the contract. Therefore, design builders should take care to provide accurate information to their lawyers for drafting their contracts.

In addition to using a contract, design/builders should take advantage of the other ways to prevent liability (Figure 6-5).

Figure 6-5. Twelve Ways to Prevent Liability Problems

- Use a well-written contract for all transactions in the construction and sales process. Both parties to the contract should read and understand all provisions before signing the document.
- Examine your insurance program and make sure it is comprehensive. Fill in any gaps in insurance coverage
- Add client's name to your general liability insurance policy.
- Ask to be listed as a "Named Insured" on the client's home owner's policy. This practice reduces your exposure to lawsuits in case a liability question should arise.
- Do not create unrealistic construction schedules.
- Follow all building codes and other regulations to the letter. Do not cut corners.
- Use reputable subcontractors and establish sound working relationships with all parties in the construction process.
- Do not make promises you cannot keep to potential buyers during the sales process nor during construction. Screen brochures, advertising, and other marketing devices for unintended promises or warranties.
- Keep customers happy and follow up quickly on punchlists and callbacks. Avoid polarization of the parties to the contract.
- Use indemnity clauses in contracts with subcontractors and design professionals.
- Disclaim implied warranties or obtain waivers of such warranties in states where such waivers are permissible.
- If all else fails, avoid going to court. Use alternative dispute resolution techniques, such as arbitration or mediation.

Source: Adapted from *Builder's Guide to Contracts and Liability* (Washington, D.C.: Home Builder Press, National Association of Home Builders, 1990), p. 5.

The Practical Construction Contract

The development of a construction contract that meets all of a design/builder's needs is a major project involving both considerable time and expense. It is the bedrock on which the company operates and must be taken seriously. However, once that up-front work is accomplished, even exceptionally long contracts can be made easy to generate, especially with a word-processing program. To create an easy-to-use contract is a matter of formatting—of differentiating between the parts of the contract that must be

---

Figure 6-6. Contract Clauses That Need Customizing

- Full legal name of each owner/buyer
- Legal description of property (lot, block, subdivision)
- Documents to be made part of the contract (plans and specifications by title, date, number of pages)
- Price of contract or if "cost plus" how that will be figured
- Allowances for owner selections
- Payout provisions (draws or percentage of completion or billings)
- Liquidated damages, if desired
- Start and completion dates
- Description of work specifications related to this project but not included in plans and specifications
- Signatures and dates ratifying contract

Figure 6-7. Contract Clauses That Can Be Standard for All Projects

- General specifications on how the design/builder builds
- General conditions on how the design/builder operates (i.e., what happens if changes are requested?)
- Clauses relating to how problems will be handled
- Right of Rescission or Cancellation
- Expiration date of contract if it is not signed

---

changed for each new client (Figure 6-6) as opposed to the parts of the contract that remain the same from project to project (Figure 6-7).

Clauses that need customizing can be kept at the beginning—except, of course, for the final signature page, which must remain at the end of the contract. With such a contract, the contract writer knows that if he/she fills in pages 1 through 3 (for example), that, except for the signature page, customizing is completed for what is perhaps a 10-page contract for a specific project.

General Specifications
Since design/builders are generating their own plans and specifications, they can standardize methods of construction. This practice saves time and money in design and in construction. Much of construction practice can be taken for granted because of this standardization. Those standard materials and methods can be spelled out in a multipage specifications section of the contract.

Normally the general specifications section would begin with a statement that unless otherwise specified differently in this particular contract, the company's standard specifications are as listed (Figure 6-8). Thus, only exceptions to the general specifications must be outlined in the customized section of the contract.

For example, the design/builder's standard drywall specifications might be "All interior partitions and ceilings will receive 1/2 inch drywall. Baths will receive 1/2 inch water-resistant (green board) drywall." Interior wall construction might be handled with a clause noting, "All new interior partitions will be built of 2x4s 16 inches on center."

Figure 6-8. Standard Specification Items

- Permits and inspections
- Excavation
- Backfilling and grading
- Footings and foundation
- Termite treatment
- Rough framing
- Masonry
- Roofing
- Gutters and downspouts
- Wall finishes
- Bath fixtures and fittings
- Venting
- Windows
- Doors
- Plumbing
- Electrical
- Heating, ventilation, and air-conditioning (HVAC)
- Insulation
- Drywall or plaster
- Ceramic tile
- Cabinets
- Appliances
- Stairs
- Painting and wallpapering
- Closet trim
- Interior and exterior trim
- Finish floors
- Carpets
- Finish hardware
- Finish grading and landscaping
- Walks and driveways
- Trash removal and site cleanliness

General Conditions

The "General Conditions" section of the construction contract describes the way the design/builder works and explains company policies in situations in which a dispute or controversy might develop. Policies properly covered in this section might include, for example, change orders, dispute handling, and warranties. Some sample questions that help pinpoint what needs to be included on these three topics appear below. Additional items usually included in this section appear with these three in the list in Figure 6-9.

Change Orders—Must they be written and signed? How will they be collected? Are they charged for in a standard way?

Dispute Handling—If a dispute related to the contract cannot be

> **Figure 6-9. Items Usually Covered in General Conditions**
>
> - Compliance with local permits and codes
> - Ownership of plans
> - Changes to work scope
> - Insurance – by design/builder and client
> - Existing hazardous materials
> - Hidden, concealed, and unforeseeable conditions
> - Dispute settlement
> - Termination and/or cancellation of contract
> - Notices – what constitutes proper notice
> - Lawyer's fee payment in event of dispute
> - Mechanic's lien provisions
> - Warranty and warranty exclusions

settled by the two parties what happens? Does it go to court? Does it go to arbitration?

Warranties—What kind of a warranty is offered for the custom home or remodeling and how long does it last and what is covered? What is not covered?

Some of the contract clauses of particular interest to design/builders are discussed below. However, this chapter is not meant to be a full treatise. A design/builder must do further research and work with a local attorney to develop a contract.

Ownership of Plans

When the design/builder has produced the blueprints for a custom home or addition and the client has them, is that client free to give or sell them to others? From a liability standpoint selling or giving them to others certainly would expose the design/builder to further risk. In addition, those plans might also have future salability for the design/builder. The following sample clause might be adapted for a design/builder's use:

> **Sample Language**
> **Builder's Plans**—The builder has provided the building plans to be used under this contract *(reference by title, date, author, and number of pages)*. Buyer has no ownership rights in the plans used under this contract. These plans are for use only by the builder, and the buyer will be liable to the builder in the amount of lost profits and all consequential damages for the reuse or resale of these plans. In addition, the builder bears no liability to anyone using these plans in violation of this contract.
>
> The builder makes no representations or warranties about the quality of these plans except those specifically provided in the limited warranty references in this contract.[1]

Defining Costs

When the builder or remodeler negotiates a "cost plus" contract with a client, those items considered costs should be spelled out in the contract. Costs as defined by the contract will be passed directly through and reimbursed by the client. Because design/builders often can charge only a minimal fee based on costs (cost plus negotiated fee) or a minimal percentage of overhead and profit (10 to 15 percent overhead and 10 percent profit), all items that can be defined as cost should be. The sample language that follows could be used for defining cost:

Sample Language

The term *cost of work* means costs necessarily incurred in builder's proper performance of the work contained in the contract documents, including the following items:

- Wages, benefits, costs of contributions and assessments for Workers' Compensation, unemployment compensation, Social Security, taxes, or any other costs incurred by the builder for labor during performance of this contract.
- Salaries for builder's personnel to the extent their time is spent on work in furtherance of completion of this contract. This payment of salaries includes (but is not limited to) work performed at shops, on the construction site, or on the road for such items as expediting the production or transporting materials or equipment.
- The builder's and the builder's agents' reasonable travel and subsistence expenses incurred in furtherance of completion of this contract.
- Payments made by the builder to subcontractors for work performed pursuant to subcontracts under this agreement.
- Cost of land and all land development expenditures associated with or apportioned to this project.
- Cost of all materials, supplies, tools, and equipment incorporated in the work and consumed in the performance of the work; cost less salvage value of such items used but not consumed that remain the property of the builder, including all costs of installing, repairing and replacing, removing, transporting, and delivering the machinery and equipment.
- Rental charges consistent with those prevailing in the area for machinery, tools, and equipment used at the construction site, whether rented from the builder or others, including all costs of installing, repairing and replacing, removing, transporting, and delivering the machinery and equipment.
- Sales, use, excise, or any other taxes related to the work imposed by governmental authorities.
- Impact fees, exactions, royalties, charges, inspection costs, or any other fees related to the work imposed by governmental authorities.
- Permit fees, royalties, or damages for infringement of patents and costs of defending related lawsuits, and deposits lost for causes other than the builder's negligence.

- Expenses for telephone service at the site, telephone calls, telegrams, postage, delivery fees, stationery, and other similar petty cash items related to work.
- Costs incurred for security at the job site.
- Costs incurred because of any emergency affecting the safety of persons or property.
- All landscaping and backfilling necessary under the contract documents, including the cost of all grading, removal or planting or trees, snow removal, frost breaking, water pumping, excavating and related work, the delivery to the site of the necessary materials, and the hauling away of excess fill and material or trash and debris.
- Builder's risk or other insurance, soil fees and civil engineering fees, performance bonds, and labor and materialmen's bonds in an amount equal to one hundred percent (100%) of the maximum costs.
- Differing site conditions, as provided for in Section 2-7 of this contract.
- Costs for preparing billing at a central/main office where it can be done most efficiently as well as costs for photocopying and printing.
- Any other costs incurred in the work that are within the scope of the work as defined in the contract documents, or any other overhead expenses.[2]

Rights of Cancellation and Rescission
Too frequently design/builders omit these two contract clauses required by federal law. However, in the event of a contract dispute, the client's attorney will first look to see what is amiss in the design/builder's contract and use that as added leverage in the dispute. The design/builder must understand these two federal regulations and comply with them when the circumstances of a particular contract require it.

The Right of Cancellation (16 CFR, Part 429) gives consumers the right to cancel a transaction within 3 business days of signing a contract if that sale was discussed or made in the consumer's home or a location other than the seller's place of business (Figure 6-10). Most remodeling and custom homebuilding transactions would fall under this law. A copy of Regulation Z, as it is often called, can be obtained from the Federal Trade Commission.

> Document Requests
> Federal Trade Commission
> Pennsylvania Avenue at 6th Street, N.W.
> Washington, D.C. 20580
> (202) 326-2222

The Right of Rescission (12 CFR, Part 226) also gives homeowners a 3-day contract cancellation period if a security interest is taken in a consumer's principal dwelling and if the contract is considered to be financed. A project with more than four payments (including change orders) is considered to be

> **Figure 6-10. Requirements of the Right of Rescission**
>
> - The contractor must deliver two copies of the right to rescind to each consumer. Thus, if two parties are owners (for example, a husband and wife, father and daughter, or two sisters), each person must receive two copies of the right to rescind.
> - The right must be presented as a separate document, not as part of a contract.
> - The right-of-rescission document must identify the transaction.
> - The document must disclose the security interest in the consumer's principal dwelling.
> - It must inform the consumer of the right to rescind the transaction.
> - The consumer must be told exactly what procedure to follow to exercise that right and must be given the form for that purpose designating the address of the creditor's (design/builder's) place of business.
> - The consumer must be told the effects of rescission.
> - The consumer must be told the date the rescission period expires.
>
> *Source:* Adapted from Figure 23-3, "Requirements of the Right of Rescission," Linda W. Case, *Remodelers Business Basics* (Washington, D.C.: National Association of Home Builders, 1989), p. 159.

financed. If the contract provides a right to lien the homeowner's property, it also falls under this federal provision.

Federal law is quite specific as to how a remodeler or custom home builder must comply. The instructions regarding the wording of contract clauses, the size of type, the number of copies, and whether it needs to be detachable must be followed precisely.

Reviewing the Contract with the Client

The contract signing meeting should always include adequate time to fully review the contract and all its provisions. In this way, the contract becomes not only a legal fall-back document, but an important tool for educating the client. This may be the first major remodeling or custom home purchase for most clients. The client does not know how the design/builder or the industry works. The signing of the contract may signal the end of the sales process, but it is only the beginning of a long and hopefully fruitful working relationship between the client and the design/builder. The proper stage is set by careful review of the particular job specifications as well as the company's general conditions of operation.

Resources

Builder's Guide to Contracts and Liability. Washington D.C.: Home Builder Press, National Association of Home Builders, 1989. 52 pp.

Case, Linda W. Chapter 22, "Contracts," and Chapter 23, "Rights of Cancellation and Rescission." *Remodelers Business Basics.* Washington, D.C. Home Builder Press, National Association of Home Builders, 1989. 232 pp.

"Right of Rescission," *Regulation Z Truth in Lending.* Washington, D.C.: Board of Governors, Federal Reserve System, 12 CFR, Part 226, April 1, 1986, amended 1981. 88 pp.

"Right of Cancellation," Cooling-Off Period for Door-to-Door Sales, 16 CFR, Part 429. Washington, D.C.: Federal Trade Commission, January 1, 1986.

What Builders and Remodelers Should Know About Right of Rescission Provisions in the Truth in Lending Act. Washington, D.C.: Consumer Affairs Department, National Association of Home Builders, 1987). 10 pp.

Notes

1. Adapted from "Sample Language," *The Builder's Guide to Contracts and Liability* (Washington, D.C.: Home Builder Press, National Association of Home Builders, 1989), p. 18.

2. Adapted from "Sample Language," *The Builder's Guide to Contracts . . .* pp. 13-14.

Production of Design/Build Projects

Design/build companies have many advantages in production (Figure 7-1). Controlling both the design as well as the construction of a project allows for control over many of the variables that can trip up a production department. Because a company spends a considerable about of time with a client during the design phase, the company develops valuable familiarity with the job and the client that can make production a smoother process. In addition, the firm has ample opportunity to obtain

---

Figure 7-1. Design/Build Advantages for Production

- The design/build firm has a long familiarity with the project. As designers and specifiers, the design/build company staff should know exactly what is needed for estimating and construction purposes.
- The company's extended working relationship with the client during sales and design should provide a good idea of the client's working style, his/her concerns, and intent. This early relationship sets the stage for a favorable working relationship during construction.
- The design/build firm is usually able to specify its preferences for 90 to 95 percent of the product selections. Thus, it prepares the way for the smooth procurement of those materials from reliable suppliers.
- The firm can make the working drawings communicate all of the information that will be needed by the field crews and subcontractors for the job. Therefore, the working drawings require constant review by those workers and feedback from them to the design department.
- When the client requests changes, they can be expeditiously put through redesign and repriced with a minimum of turnaround time.
- The company designers can draw the project details and the building methods in the way preferred by the production department. The design/builder thus controls the myriad of blueprint details that combine to make a construction job. With this level of standardization in construction, field workers can become more efficient and productive.

advice and suggestions from production personnel regarding production methods, systems, and materials to improve design, reduce labor costs, and keep estimating accurate.

Every design/build firm reaps some production benefits from the combined design-construction process. How many design/build firms take full advantage of these positive effects in production? In the author's experience, amazingly few. Design/build firms often focus primarily on the sales and marketing impact of this operating mode. However, the production benefits listed in Figure 7-1 do not just happen automatically. The company must take action to make them happen.

Service Businesses

All businesses are service businesses. Some are just more so. Design/build of one-of-a-kind residential projects is heavily service-oriented. Design/build remodelers and custom home builders sell both service and product, but the service is a lion's share of the package. In service businesses, the final delivery of the product (a new addition or a new, custom built home) is extremely important. However, the process through which that product delivery is accomplished is equally important.

The custom home or remodeling project may be beautifully and masterfully built. However, if the client had an unpleasant relationship with the builder throughout construction, new prospects will be referred elsewhere by that client.

Remodelers and custom home builders must deliver top technical quality as a base from which to operate. If they are design/build companies, they must also deliver excellent design services. However, unless they can accomplish these two tasks in a reliable, user-friendly way, they will not be successful in their businesses.

The design/build client often is on the scene at every step. Frequently this project provides the client's first experience with building, blueprints, and a myriad of choices in product, finish, selections. The client is anxious, proud, concerned. A large part of the design/build firm's job is to walk the client through the process in a friendly, helpful, consultative fashion.

The production department of a design/build firm is the prime deliverer of service. Field employees and subcontractors commonly focus on technical proficiency and quality, and design/build companies should stress to these employees that how that quality is achieved is of prime importance both to the client and to the success of the business. Friendliness, helpfulness, neatness, and reliability all become critically important. All field employees must fully understand their roles in that service. In addition, all of the subcontractors on the job must be able to deliver at least moderate levels of service, friendliness, and reliability. This aspect of customer service is even more difficult for the design/builder to control. The "Working Together" memo to subconstractors in Figure 7-2 helps to promote a cooperative attitude that pays off in terms of customer service.

Figure 7-2. Memo of Instructions to Subcontractors

John Cable Architects • Builders
Associates, Inc.

311 S. Washington Street
Alexandria, Virginia 22314

(703) 683-6676
FAX 683-6740

John H. Cable, AIA
President

To:
Date:
RE: Working Together

Congratulations on being selected as a participant on the JOHN CABLE Associates design/build "team". Our relationship with you will be established and maintained because of a mutual commitment to quality and customer satisfaction. There are some basic administrative requirements that we have established in order to do business together. Let's address each one separately:

(1) Proposals: We need to know what our subcontractor costs will be before we sign a contract with a client. At some point in our bidding/negotiating process, we will request a written proposal from you. It is important to describe in detail not only what you are including, but also what you are **not** including in this price. Comprehensive details at this point will prevent potential misunderstandings later in the job. Proposals should include the draw schedule you are requesting.

(2) Change Orders: In general, we want to keep these to a minimum. The client hates getting them from us and we don't like getting them from you. If a change order is merited, we need to be notified as soon as you know about it. The additional work is **not** to be done until we accept the change order, preferably in writing. Any change order should contain a description of the additional work to be done, as well as the price agreed to. If it is impossible to determine a set price, a "not to exceed" price should be assigned to the work.

(3) Site Conditions: In general, JCA will provide the hauling of any scrap materials from the site. However, it is the sole responsibility of each sub to pick up his/her trash daily and place it in the designated collection area. Should you fail to do so, JCA will back charge the contract three percent (3%) of the total contract price.

If you need to store materials which you are supplying, check with the lead carpenter to determine the best place for them. We assume no responsibility for materials which you choose to store at our site. If, on the other hand, we supply the materials that you will be installing, we are responsible for maintaining them up until the time we hand them over to you. At that point, you will be asked to replace any items which you break, damage, or lose.

(4) Billing: Draw schedules outlined on your proposals are very helpful. This way we can predict the flow of cash required for that particular job. We ask that you submit an invoice for the amount that is due upon completion of the relevant phase of work. Since our payables operation is computerized, we find that this is necessary to ensure that we flag payment to you on time. Typically, draw amounts should be tied in with progress on the job (at rough-in, at trim-out, etc. for example).

Source: Reprinted with permission from John Cable, AIA, president, John Cable Associates, Inc., Alexandria, Virginia.

Figure 7-2. Memo of Instructions to Subcontractors (Continued)

Checks are printed once a week on Thursday afternoons. In order to be entered on time and considered for payment, we must have your invoice in hand the preceding week. Checks will be mailed out on Friday morning. If you want to pick up your check here at the office, you must let us know by Thursday at 5:00 PM.

(5) Information: We need to keep some basics on file, like the complete name of your business, your federal I.D. number or your social security number, your mailing address, and all of your phone numbers where it is possible to reach you (office, beeper, car, etc.). Please provide this information to us.

(6) Insurance: JCA requires that all its subcontractors carry their own coverage for both liability and workers compensation. We need a certificate of insurance on file to show to our insurance company when they do their annual audit. If we do not have such a certificate for you, we will be required to pay the premium for the amount that we paid you during that policy year. Please contact your agent immediately and have them send a certificate of insurance to us at the address listed above as soon as possible. Please be sure your coverage is valid for the state in which our job(s) is(are) located. If you do not have the required insurance and we decide to do business with you anyway, we will deduct from your check any amount that we will have to pay when audited.

(7) Communication: This may well be the most important skill that you need in order to continue our working relationship. There is nothing more frustrating than leaving messages on a machine for three days before a call is returned. In general, we need to have you available to answer questions and respond to emergency situations. The ability to leave a message that will get a prompt response is a must. Also, if you tell us that you will be on a job site on a certain date and/or time, we will expect that to happen. If you find that the situation has changed on your end, we need to know it as soon as you do. This is critical in shifting our scheduling around.

In closing, we strive for very positive relationships with each of our subcontractors. You are viewed by our clients as a representative of our team. We like to get the job done well and have a good time doing it. JCA will always be available to work with you to provide appropriate conditions to facilitate your process. In return we ask that you do the same for us. If we can support your success and growth while you support ours, we will be doing business in the kind of win-win environment that we are looking for.

Sincerely,

John H. Cable
President

Source: Reprinted with permission from John Cable, AIA, president, John Cable Associates, Inc., Alexandria, Virginia.

Transition from Sales to Production

Once a client signs the construction contract, the salesperson needs to package the project for production. Invariably the client file contains scraps of paper, rejected sketches, material that can be thrown out or filed elsewhere. Some firms use a job file checklist to be sure that no crucial action or form is missed (Figure 7-3). The salesperson turns a copy of the checklist and a copy of each item in the file over to the production department. The original of each item, including the checklist, is also retained in the office file.

The estimate of construction costs must be revised to reflect any final changes. The estimate must be completely clear to the production manager who will buy the needed products and services based on it. Usually the estimate incorporates a cover summary sheet with the different categories contained in the estimate, the line item cost for that phase, and numerous backup sheets of the details that comprise the individual line items. The production manager must be able to buy everything for the job—materials, labor, and subcontractors—from the estimate.

The working drawings may need some redrawing in order to reflect changes resulting from final negotiation with the client. Most projects will have changes throughout construction that will tamper with the integrity of the blueprints, but the job should start with a fully accurate set of drawings.

Because design is so readily available in a design/build firm, out-of-date plans sometimes are inadvertently used on a jobsite by a subcontractor who is unaware of the more recent revision. This situation can lead to expensive mistakes. One of the first steps the production manager should take is to see that all subcontractors are equipped with the latest revision of the blueprints.

When the transition of a job from sales into production is poorly handled, the design/build company is already behind before it begins the job. Future mistakes are already built into the process. A constant feedback loop between sales and production assures that production personnel can evaluate the new project packet and request further clarification or details.

Most salespeople are either company owners or on commission and want to see a happy client, an accurate estimate, and an on-time schedule. Thus, they should be highly motivated to see that production personnel are armed for success with all the information they need to complete the project.

Strong Field Leadership

Design/build remodelers are most likely to have carpenters and helpers on staff as employees. Custom home builders are more likely to subcontract carpentry. Both remodelers and custom builders will have an in-house, construction supervisor although in smaller companies that is likely to be the owner—and only one of the owner's many job functions.

No matter how carpentry on a project is accomplished, it is the central and most important of the various specialties because it comprises the largest labor expenditure and because carpentry

102 Design/Build

Figure 7-3. Sample Job Folder Checklist

From Concept to Completion

LARSEN
BUILDERS

Job Folder Checklist
TSI 101

JOB NAME: START DATE
ADDRESS: PROJECTED FINISH

JOB FOLDER CHECKLIST
- Proposal
- Specifications
- Right of Recission
- Standard Conditions
- Warantee
- Plans
- Permits
- Fees
- Selections
- Special Orders
- Before Pictures
- Original Estimate
- Schedule
- Sub Contract Agreements
- Material Lists
- Job Cost Budget vs Actual
- Pre-Construction Conference
- Allowance Worksheet
- Master Crew Schedule
- Timesheets
- Change-Orders
- Client Responsibility
- Walk-Thru Punch-Out
- Production Evaluation

DO BEFORE JOB STARTS
- Obtain Job Folder from Sales
- Review Job Folder Information
- On-site inspection with Salesman
- Plan Approval
- Engineering Checks
- Pull Permit, pay any fees
- Write up all material lists
- Put material lists out for bid
- Write up all sub agreements
- Put sub contracts out for bid
- Write up Gantt schedule
- Have all sub agreements signed
- Write up Job Cost Budget / Actual
- Order Specialty Items
- Give Job Cost Budget to Office
- Order dumpster, obtain any permit
- Be sure all selections made
- Schedule Construction Start
- Assign crews to Master Schedule
- Set up job phone, job signs
- Pull temporary utilities
- Pre-Construction Conference
- Put up fence, job box, first-aid
- All special orders are delivered

SPECIAL ORDER ITEMS

SELECTIONS MADE

NOTES

Source: Reprinted with permission from Don Larsen, president, Larsen Builders, Alameda, California.

"weaves" through the entire project from start to finish. When the company employs its own lead carpenters, one of these working, project carpenters oversees the entire job. If the lead carpenter is part of a subcontracted crew, the networking of the various job facets and responsibilities must be done by the production manager.

Leading-edge design/builders bring the production manager and lead carpenter or carpentry subcontractor into the planning and estimating process. When the builder bids out carpentry to a number of subs, this early involvement may not be feasible. However, the winning subcontractor's comments and suggestions can be obtained and assessed at the point the contract is awarded.

In-House Carpentry

Design/builders who employ carpenters take on a considerable risk of labor overruns. They do not have the assurance of a fixed carpentry price. In fact, they have a running carpentry meter, and the final tab will not be known until the punchlist is finished. Because labor dollars are spent from the job, the lead carpenter needs to be educated on job costing and comparison of those estimates with actual costs. Some tips for design/build cost control are listed in Figure 7-4.

When carpentry is subcontracted, the design/builder should search for carpentry subs with which to develop a long-term

---

Figure 7-4. Tips for Design/Build Cost Control

- Bring the carpenter into the design development and working drawing stages of planning (possible only in the design/build company). The carpenter's input is invaluable on how to design for construction efficiency, detailing, pricing. While they are giving their input, they should be learning the complete set of time goals for every carpentry activity on the jobsite. Many carpenters have no concept of how job costing is done, but once they learn they can work to meet these time (or dollar) goals on various phases of construction.

- Give the carpenter labor estimates for various job phases and ask for help in developing ideas for saving carpentry time and effort on the jobsite. Give him/her frequent job cost printouts on actual time expended (at least monthly). Discuss how to read job cost reports and review the expenditures still to be expected.

- When the job is completed, do a "postmortem" review of it with the carpenter and production manager. What could have been better designed, more efficiently designed? What job decisions led to errors and rework? How can the next job be done more efficiently?

- Share the "winnings" with the lead carpenter and crew. Develop a performance-based job bonus to share dollar savings from the labor predicted in the estimate. Many companies give the crew 50 percent of labor dollars saved with the lead carpenter getting the lion's share. Pay out the bonus as quickly as possible. The production manager's bonus should come from the company's 50 percent of these savings.

relationship. A custom builder may have two or three such subcontractors. This type of relationship which still allows for competitive bidding, facilitates early input on jobs in design, which is so critical for design/builders.

Improving Buildability

Bringing the lead carpenter or carpentry subcontractor into a complete feedback loop with design and estimating has three major purposes:

- Designing for ease, construction efficiency, and practicality, which impact costs and function
- Estimating those costs accurately by consulting with the person spending the labor dollars
- Constant input as to which subcontractors and suppliers are performing well and which are not

The design/builder also should solicit early input on design from the major subcontractors and, after the project is completed, ask for their suggestions for improving the next job. In this way, the design/builder has an active program to continue to improve the buildability of its designs. When design and construction are housed under the same roof with constant feedback from both functions, the client is well served, the production department runs smoothly, and the job costs become accurate.

Strong Client Management

The excellent client relationship developed through design will be tested in construction—especially in remodeling. Custom home builders differ over whether to welcome the client to drop by the jobsite unannounced. Some welcome any visit. Others prefer that the client schedule such an appointment. Almost all custom home builders agree that they do not want the client talking to job personnel other than the production manager.

Since the client lives on the remodeling site, remodelers have no such choice. The client has full access to all production personnel, and therefore, the remodeler's team must be socially skilled. They need to be personable—polite, friendly, and helpful. Those same characteristics are required for the subcontractors and their personnel as well. Because the crew is "living" with the client, free and open communication with all personnel is common on a remodeling site. Some restrictions are enforced, however, particularly that no pricing can be given directly to the owner by the subcontractor or the carpenter. Other restrictions involve a dress code, treating the customer with respect (no smoking, no radios, no foul language) and other elements of customer service (Figure 7-5). Normally, the lead carpenter or working job foreperson acts as the main communicator with the client. Often this person qualifies for an incentive bonus if the job is brought in successfully—with high marks on customer service and with the job either at or under budget.

Figure 7-5. Job Work Rules

Some remodelers, especially those doing large, whole-house renovations strongly urge their client to move out, rent temporary living quarters, and store their furniture. This practice often saves the remodeler money, time, and effort because no one has to work around a family and its furnishings.

Each design/builder needs to develop a process that informs the client about job progress, that gets selections and changes processed in the proper time frame, and that takes the client's "temperature" daily to be sure they are satisfied with the job and the production process.

Site Walkthrough

In many design/build companies, the lead carpenter and production manager will have some familiarity with a job before the sale. However, after the contract has been signed, production will begin to focus on learning all pertinent information needed to construct the project.

In remodeling, a lot of that information is obtained during a jobsite walkthrough to assess existing conditions, determine site access, and review the plans. This walkthrough is normally conducted by the salesperson or designer and includes the production manager and the lead carpenter (or carpentry subcontractor). Figure 7-6 provides two pages of a design/builder's five-page job set-up form to assist the production manager in organizing the production of the job. Page two includes a checklist for such a site walkthrough.

Client Education

The long and careful client relationship developed during the sales and design process is also carefully tended during production when the greatest stress is placed on the client.

Design/builders should consider instituting a preconstruction conference with the client to review the contract provisions and specifications. The preconstruction conference sets the stage for smooth teamwork during construction. The production manager usually conducts this meeting, which also includes the salesperson and lead carpenter (or carpentry subcontractor). The assembled group reviews exactly what is being constructed as well as what is not included in the contract. If the client has any changes, any misunderstandings, or any concerns, all the parties involved can hear them.

In addition to reviewing the scope of the job, the production manager reviews the company's process for accomplishing the construction work. The discussion of this process with the client should include an explanation of who does what in the design/build company, who the client should work with, how the client can make changes and voice complaints or concerns, when draws will be due and how they are paid.

While clients have on-going access to the design/builder's time when needed, setting up a standard weekly meeting between

Figure 7-6. Design/Build Site Checklist

From Concept to Completion

LARSEN BUILDERS

Design/Build Site Checklist
TSI 200

Job Name:

PLAN REVIEW, PHASE I | Check

Lay out major dimensions (in red) on set of floor plans or on foundation plan (this will verify plan dimensions internally and externally and provide measurements for foundation layout). Don't forget to establish sub-floor reference height	
Check foundation details, waste lines, plumbing and electrical. Feeds, vent locations access holes, piers, saddles, anchors, J-belt locations (mark on plan in green)	
Establish center lines and rough openings for all doors and windows, and other specific framed details such as built-ins, stairs, beams, roof windows, arches, hallways, toilet niches, medicine cabinets, shower layouts, curbs, drains, glass partitions (mark on plan in red)	
Assess details, missing information, consistency between drawing, reference points and conflicts	
Check all cabinets and details for subcontractor reference or attention (mark on plan in yellow)	
Source tear sheets for all appliances and fixtures as well as samples of tile, trim, etc.	
Identify all structural special order items and verify during discovery process of earlier, then order (mark plan in yellow)	
Assemble materials list, break down into phase-by-phase packages. Identify suppliers (cost-shop if possible)	
List all sub-contractor and by-owner down by phase and lead time (mark on plan in yellow)	

TAKE-OFFS AND DELIVERY SCHEDULE | Check

Framing Lumber, Trusses, Beams	
Window/Door Order (establish rough opening)	
Siding	
Exterior Trim and Mill Work	
Interior Trim and Mill Work	
Cabinet as-built dimensions (check w/subcontractor)	
Insulation	
Sheetmetal Flashings	
Sheetmetal Sub-work (Scope)	
Drywall, etc.	
Finish Flooring	
Subfloor/Underlayment	
Tile Substrates (mortar beds, backer board heights, tile thicknesses, etc.) & Alignments. Get samples for size & thickness	
Wall, Ceiling and Floor Finishes, Thicknesses	
Appliance and Lighting Tearsheets	
Details, Mock-ups, Other unusual conditions and information, contractor-initiated changes and substitutions	

Source: Reprinted with permission from Don Larsen, president, Larsen Builders, Alameda, California.

Figure 7-6. Design/Build Site Checklist (Continued)

SUBCONTRACTOR INFORMATION — Check

Shop Drawings
Locations (ducts, fixtures, etc.)
Appliance Tearsheets
Timeframes for work; special sequencing
Specifications

SITE VISIT #1 — Check

Assess site for access, scaffolding and craning requirements, debris handling
Identify staging and storage areas
Identify work-only areas and tool storage, deliver tool cabinet
Lay out any string lines required. Establish heights for foundation or interior work (counter tops, window sills, etc.)
Arrange for phone hookup, fax location, if required. Lock box for keys
Post "No Parking" signs for debris box
Verify or arrange for toilet facilities and sink, if possible
Order intitial material delivery and determine crew strength at start-up
Power and water, Lights
establish reference points, level lines, batter boards
Post job card and safe keep permit and permit plan set
Job kit (plans, permit, first aid, scale, pencils, pens, time cards, phone, phone books, supplier list & phone numbers

PLAN REVIEW, PHASE II (ON SITE) — Check

Identify all areas requiring discovery. Develop methods/procedures for dealing with same and sketch or note in job folder (mark on plan in yellow)
Identify all entry points and chase locations for services, flues, ducts, etc. (mark on plan in green)
Verify wall and roof framing details. Establish accurate plate heights, sill and header heights on plans in red. Check roof pitches, stair run-outs, as required
Check (E) floors for level and establish reference location. Mark on structure (mark on plan in red)
Establish demo sequence and identify salvage items

DEMO (E) STRUCTURE AS REQUIRED FOR WALL FRAMING, SUB-CONTRACTORS DISCOVERY — Check

Laborers
Dumpster (place "No Parking" signs in advance)
Debris chute

Source: Reprinted with permission from Don Larsen, president, Larsen Builders, Alameda, California.

production manager and client can be beneficial. The client often lists any questions and changes to discuss at the meeting, and at least once a week, the production manager is able to update the schedule for the client, ask any questions, and get change orders signed. Clients are often less anxious about the process if they believe the remodeler or builder will stay in touch with them and keep them involved in the process.

As the project nears completion, a precompletion punchlist should be scheduled so that the client and production manager can walk through the house or remodeling project to catch any last items which need repair or replacement. The design/builder should view the walkthrough, not only as a practical checkout procedure, but also as a chance to resell the client on the beauty of the client's choices and the wisdom of the decision to build.[1] The walkthrough provides an opportunity to discuss what the company might have done better in its delivery of service, what the client particularly likes about the design, which personnel did outstanding work, and which fell down or faltered in delivering service or product.

Product Selections

In custom homebuilding and (to a lesser extent) in remodeling, one of the most difficult production problems is getting all customer selections and allowances closed in a timely fashion. Today's client is most of all short of time. Yet the client's choices may involve long lead times because they must be special ordered. The smart design/builder controls this selection process with a firm but friendly hand.

A number of companies include time with an interior designer to take care of and facilitate these choices. Other companies include a half day of an employee's time to take the client to the various showrooms. Without any guidance, clients often go off track and choose materials that will not fit, will not match, or that present technical problems for the design/builder. By turning what could be a production problem into a sellable asset ("Your contract includes a half day to visit showrooms with our interior designer and his/her help in making selections and coordinating colors and styles."), the design/builder is truly making lemonade when presented with lemons.

Design/builders who make these shopping alliances with a designer normally pay a flat fee. Thus, the heavy shopper's hourly costs balance off the light shopper's. Sometimes this flat fee is priced economically by the designer because the designer may be able to sell the client curtains, carpet, furniture, and accessories. Most interior designers are happy to have access to a client who is just moving into a new home or a new addition. The client, the design/builder, and the interior designer all win in this relationship.

A form listing the selections made, the vendors, vendors' phone numbers, and other needed information helps to keep track of these selections (Figure 7-7).

The design/builder without such an alliance should develop a

Figure 7-7. Sample Design/Build Selection

VRANIZAN
DESIGN/BUILD
Building Distinction by Design

Selection Sheet
TSI 310

Date _____

Client: _____ Address: _____ City: _____ Phone: _____

ITEM		VENDOR	PHONE #	JOBBER	PHONE #
Wallpaper					
Drapes					
Carpet					
Ceramic Tile					
Kitchen Tile					
Bath Tile					
Flooring					
Fans					
Blinds					
Lighting					
Area Carpet					
Wood Stoves					
Cabinet Stains					
Wall Paint					
Formica					
Marble					
Appliances					
Furniture					
Hot Tubs					
Cabinet Acces.					
Paintings					
Plants					
Windows					
Mirrors					

Source: Reprinted with permission from Bob Vranizan, president, Vranizan Design/Build, San Francisco, California.

form for the client (Figure 7-8) that lists electrical, plumbing, paint, carpet, wallpaper, and cabinet showrooms with addresses, phone numbers, and hours as well as the salesperson who services that design/builder. This form should include space to list what needs to be selected and the date by which the selection is due.

Figure 7-8. Sample Entry for Client's Selection

Plumbing Fixtures Select by: _____(date)_____

Mary Doe, Salesperson
ZYX Plumbing Supply
444 Main Street
Anytown, Any State, U.S.A.
(000) 333-4444

Showroom Hours: 8 a.m.-4 p.m., weekdays
                10 a.m.-2 p.m., Saturdays
To be selected:

_____
_____
_____
_____

Remember to take the blueprints with you to this showroom.

However selections are handled, clients tend to be late in making choices if the design/builder does not create a system in which they are constantly reminded that a decision is due. Simply hoping it will happen correctly does not assure prompt product choices.

Allowances for Product Selections

In order to close a contract within a reasonable time frame and before all product choices are made, both custom home builders and remodelers commonly include allowances for those selections in the contract. Thus, a clause may, for example, give the client $7,000 for carpeting or $18,000 for cabinetry. Normally, these allowances are marked up at the bottom line of the estimate so that the amount shown as an allowance is to be used to pay the actual bill of the selection.

In handling allowances, companies differ on whether they give the client the list price on the item or the firm's discounted price. That decision is one each design/builder must make. A second decision determines how the firm will handle overages or underages on the selections.

If the client selects something less expensive than the allowance would provide, does the client receive a credit only for the actual difference between the selection and the allowance, or is the client also refunded some markup? The most common way design/

builders handle underexpended money is to refund back the credit only from the allowed amount.

A more frequent problem occurs when the client spends more than the allowance. This problem is one of great controversy among remodelers and custom home builders. Some design/builders simply charge the client the amount of the actual selection overage with no markup, assuming no extra work was caused. Thus, if the client is allowed $3,000 in the contract to purchase 25 light fixtures and actually spends $4,500 doing so, the client receives a charge for the additional $1,500. These design/builders would contend that charging overhead and profit on the excess often angers the client who believes it is unfair.

Other design/builders strongly believe that they should receive at least a minimal markup on the overage for overhead and profit. Indeed, the cost of liability insurance is often based on receipts, and if a commission is being paid to a real estate agent who referred the client and that commission is based on total billings, that extra $1,500 involves some real costs.

One solution to obtaining markup is use of the list price as the amount charged back against the allowance. When the design/builder charges the client list price for the selection under an allowance but receives a discounted price, that allows some markup automatically to the builder or remodeler. A firmly established, written company policy on this issue can reduce the potential for conflict with clients and make sure that each client is treated alike.

Client Changes

Design/build companies have an advantage in redesign. Design changes can be fully accomplished quickly and by their own personnel. However, most design/builders would agree that the best-run jobs have a minimum of changes. Nevertheless, the client who has chosen to build or remodel in such a custom manner cannot be denied the ability to change the work. In fact, many clients are not good at reading blueprints and only know when they see the walls going up what they really want. The answer is a careful balance of contractor and client interests. Changes are inevitable, but they can be controlled. Careful delineation of a client's needs during sales and design will fit the project to the client with a minimum of redesign. Control of change orders actually begins in sales.

Design/Build's Impact on Production

The most unsung advantages of design/build lie in its positive effect on production. However, not enough companies fully utilize the benefits of designing construction efficiency into the project, as well as the tremendous advantage of having the lead carpenter's and the production manager's input into design and estimating.

The production department of every design/build firm should be the company's most important marketing tool. The referrers of future business to the company—today's client—will either be won or lost depending on the service received while that client's project is under construction. The service delivered by a design/build firm's construction department can ultimately determine whether that firm thrives or fails.

Note

1. For more information see Carol Smith, *The Positive Walkthrough: Your Blueprint for Success* (Washington, D.C.: National Association of Home Builders, 1990), 139 pp.

8

Residential Design/Build for Remodelers

Design/build in remodeling (where design is isolated and paid for as a separate professional service) began as a small scattered trend in the 1970s. The owners of some large remodeling firms tired of providing free design only to see their prospective buyers go to cheaper remodelers for construction and began charging for their design services.

Often these early charges were in the range of 1 to 2 percent of construction budget, but they served to qualify the client as a serious buyer. Charging for the design of a remodeling job meant the remodeler worked with serious buyers, had a longer time period in which to sell the client on the firm, and if the client "walked" before signing a construction contract, the remodeler at least broke even financially on the services provided.

Design/build has been an active trend in remodeling in the 80s. An estimated 20 percent of full-line remodelers with volumes of $1 million plus are packaging their services as design/build. In companies under $1 million in volume, probably 5 percent run a design/build operation. An NAHB survey[1] of professional remodelers shows that in-house design services are offered by 70 percent of the respondents. However, not all of those companies charge for the design service.

Design/build remodelers tend to stress the construction end of the business and to use design as a "chute" into selling their construction services. Their design charges now average 3 to 4 percent of the construction budget in comparison with 10 to 15 percent for design-only architectural services in their communities. Compared with custom home builders and architects in design/build, they are more likely to rebate at least part of the design fee if the client signs a construction contract.

For the remodeler, probably the greatest benefit of design/build is that it nearly eliminates competitive bidding for construction. Because the client agrees to the price up front, as long as that budget is met, the client is ready to move directly into construction. However, if the estimate based on the working drawings exceeds the budget, and the client has not been kept up-to-date financially, the client will tend to try to keep to the original budget by competitively bidding the project rather than move directly into construction with the design/build firm.

The level of design capability and the professionalism of the services provided by remodelers varies from superb to primitive. This type of purchase is clearly made by an upper-middle class client demographically, so the proposal should be well packaged and implemented by the remodeler.

Becoming a design/build remodeler adds a marketing burden to the company. Every project, brochure, business card, and salesperson will be evaluated by the consumer based, not only on, "Does this firm know how to build?" but also on "How well will this company carry out and enhance my design ideas?" Despite some drawbacks, design/build has proven to be a tremendous advance for remodelers. It allows them to take control of the client process and move out of the highly competitive, cutthroat world of selling remodeling based only on price.

The following two interviews illustrate two company approaches to design/build remodeling. Each company owner has devised a basically sound system using many of the principles espoused in this book. Yet, in a number of instances, their practices are something other than the textbook answer. The interviews are meant to give depth and reality to theory. They are intended to show the "real" company in action rather than the "perfect" company.

An Interview with David Johnston

Company Profile

Business: Design/build remodeling
Years in business: 7
1989 volume: $1.8 million
Number of jobs in 1989: 35
Average job size: $51,000
Personnel:
  Office—2 partners, 1 receptionist, 1 1/2 bookkeepers, 2 architect-salespeople
  Field—3 production managers, 15 carpenters

Figure 8-1. David Johnston and his partner Eric Havens

Source: Reprinted with permission from May 1989 issue of *Remodeling* magazine, copyright (c) Hanley-Wood, Inc.

Company History

I studied under Buckminster Fuller at Southern Illinois University and got my degree in environmental systems design, which was really passive solar design and construction management. After I graduated I consulted with the National Park Service on solar and energy conservation issues in the parks, worked with the U.S. Department of Energy on its solar program as a liaison between the construction industry and the government.

In 1980 I founded the National Passive Solar Industries Council, which is still alive and well today. I stayed on the federal "dole" until the Republican Administration dismantled many of the programs on which I was working.

I decided I wanted to build some solar buildings rather than talk about them. I started Lightworks to be a solar remodeling company. From my national perspective during the 1980s, I saw that remodeling was the most stable segment of the construction industry and that the Washington, D.C., area was a particularly stable market.

My degree was truly a design/build degree, so that was the approach I took in my own business. I had no capital. After 6 months, Derek Havens, now my minority partner in the business, joined me. Derek, a long-time friend with an art history and education degree, had been pursuing an art career and paying the bills by working in construction. Derek wanted to design, and I said I'd do the selling. We've learned a lot in our 7 years in this business.

The Design/Build Process

When a prospective client calls us, we ask the usual questions: What is the scope of the work they want done? Do they have plans already? If so, we ask them to send those plans to us to examine and then we decide whether we want to bid them or not. In general, we do not like to do that kind of bidding. We ask: How many other contractors are they talking with? How did they happen to call us? Out of 10 calls, 2 will have already consulted an architect, 4 will know they want to use a design/build approach, and 4 don't have a clue about what they are doing.

We are not good at qualifying—by choice. We do try to stay with jobs over $10,000 with a few exceptions. We'll do a smaller job if it's for a former client, if it is an entre to a valuable future client, or if it is an intriguing job. Of 10 leads, we'll proceed to a first visit with 7 or 8. We'll ultimately close a construction contract with 1 out of 4 people we meet for that first visit (or 2 out of the original 10 calls).

During this initial phone conversation, we'll explain how our design/build business operates and that after some free, up-front consultation, the client must sign and pay for the design stages. We set up a first home site visit with those who survive this phone interview.

First Appointment

[Partner Derek Havens speaking]

I walk the existing house with the client. I try to extract a budget figure from the prospect—sometimes the client has set one, sometimes not. We talk about what they want and whether what they want is really what they need. Then I give them some idea of the budget range they should be considering. I try to shoot high on that.

If my budget figure is too high for the client, I try to salvage it by cutting the scope of the project.

I give the prospect a promotional package of materials (our brochure, my card, reprints of articles about the company (Figure 8-2), all in a distinctive high-gloss, purple presentation folder with our logo on it). I explain that the next step is a design contract and what that will cost. I ask if they want to give me their go-ahead now or whether they would like to think about it and call me.

Our first visit is not a hard sell. In fact we just don't believe in a hard sell. I'm trying to give the prospects enough information to make their decisions. I solicit trust. I sell myself as someone they can communicate with. If they feel comfortable with me, the chances are that they will get back in touch.

If I suspect that some of these are potential problem clients, probably because of bad chemistry between us, these people will often weed themselves out.

We're selling service and a process keyed into the client's budget, taste, need. We are eliciting business rather than closing business.

The Design Contract

We have a three-stage design process. Conceptual design drawings, soft-line drawings, and working drawings. We charge hourly and ask for a retainer up front on each stage. We bill every week against that retainer. That billing covers both drawing and estimating. On a $100,000 addition, our charges would run $5,000 to $10,000.

We keep the design stages purposely loose, so a client can easily get out of it if he/she wants. But we do use a written contract. We ask the client to make a "wish list" of details for the projects. We may not be able to build all of them into the budget, but we get

Figure 8-2. Magazine Article Reprint and Promotion Piece

Source: Reprinted with permission from May 1989 issue of *Remodeling* magazine, copyright (c) Hanley-Wood, Inc.

some idea of what is important to the client.

Our first design stage is working up two or three conceptual drawings that might solve their space problems.

In the second stage, soft-line layouts, we work out many of the finish details and give the client a preliminary construction estimate based on those plans. The plans are quite complete as far as letting the clients know what they are getting—for instance, cabinet elevations—but they still aren't full working drawings with all the information the lead carpenter needs.

The third stage is preparing full working drawings, full specifications, a final price, and a construction contract for the client. We like to give the client a good estimate of how much this stage will cost.

We share office space with an architectural firm and that has given us a chance to see how these architects work and to learn how to produce more sophisticated plans and design services. I do try to make our drawings economical for the client. Since we will be building them ourselves, have implied standards of quality, and use known construction techniques, they don't have to be 110 percent complete. As a design/build firm, we're not oriented toward monuments to our design nor toward architectural statements. We really try to meet the client's needs in a way that is harmonious with the existing house and the available budget.

We think design/build should be a seamless process. Architecture has to be functional art. If it isn't functional for the client, then we have failed. Many of our clients have been burned by working with architects. Sometimes they come to us when they find their plans are for projects that are 200 percent over their stated budgets, and we redraw to fit the scope to the budget.

Marketing

[David Johnston again]

Our marketing focuses on a number of activities. Referrals provide 50 percent of our new clients. As we get bigger, that percentage has trouble keeping up and seems to supply fewer leads proportionately.

We believe in networking in the community. We get a consistent flow of leads from our participation in the Chamber of Commerce, from an entrepreneur's group to which we belong, and from keeping a high social profile in our communities.

Site signs are a steady source of leads. One of our surprise sources of leads this year has been our two spec rehabbed houses we have on the market. Many potential home buyers have come to us and asked us to help them find a house to rehab for their own. Neighbors of our rehabs have called us. Our open houses have generated a number of calls for remodeling.

We are really pushing publicity for the company. We have a regular remodeling column in a good-looking Capitol Hill newspaper and have had articles published in other neighborhood papers.

Five-Year Plan

I see Lightworks being a multifaceted corporation with remodeling representing one division along with commercial renovation. I also see a strong push toward development of our own projects—both residential and commercial. We are also considering spinning off design services as a profit-making entity.

Figure 8-3. The Johnston/Havens Philosophy

- Design and construction are one continuous process, and that process is successful when the client is left happy.
- We are in a service—not product—business. If we forget that, we will shoot ourselves in the foot. Service can be difficult to sell initially because it's abstract and because every company can make promises. The service can be identified only in retrospect. Therefore, third-party endorsements (referrals) are important.
- We are explicit in our win-win approach to business. Both parties must get what they want in the transaction.
- We are in this business to make a profit. We do not keep this a secret. We are not shy about letting our clients know that we need a 5 percent net profit. Some people believe us, some don't.
- We like to transact business in a participatory way. We engage our clients in the process. We include our employees in this participation.
- Above all, we believe in having fun. "Controlled abandon" is our byword. When everyone agrees to the control structure and that the project is preeminent, we can have fun within that structure.
- We have no problems, only solutions, on the job. When everyone is participating to put the best interests of the project above personal best interests, solutions become obvious.
- Our true contract with our clients is an attitudinal one—not a written one.

An Interview with Tom Mullen, CR

Company Profile

Business: Residential and commercial contractor doing design/build remodeling
Years in Business: 8
1989 volume: $700,000
Number of 1989 jobs: 12
Average job size: $60,000
Personnel:
  Office—Owner and 1 office manager/accountant
  Field—4 working foremen

Figure 8-4. Tom Mullen, president of Doubletree Construction, Scottsdale, Arizona

Company History

I have a varied work history and over the years I've gotten three associate degrees—social science, agribusiness, accounting.

In the 1970s I was living in San Diego managing operations for a rock-and-roll radio station, promoting concerts, and serving as a general partner in a production company.

These activities led to a pivotal experience. I was part of a group of investors who bought an old vaudeville theater and turned it into a concert hall and theater with adjacent shops and restaurant. Suddenly, I found myself very interested in the renovation.

By 1974 my wife Donna and I had settled in Oregon. We changed lifestyles altogether. We were living in a house I designed and built on a small farm. I went back to school and got my second degree—in agribusiness. On the side I was buying and rehabbing houses to rent or resell. I also designed and built a new type of laundry facility as well. All of a sudden, I realized I was again working 50 to 60 hours a week, plus farming.

By 1980 Donna and I had moved to Phoenix, Arizona, where Donna had many relatives. I started out buying, renovating, and selling homes in the hot Phoenix market. I specialized, and still do, in Paradise Valley, a high-income community near Scottsdale and Phoenix.

While I waited for my houses to sell, I began doing jobs for other real estate agents. (I am also a real estate broker.) I then opened Doubletree Construction with a partner in early 1982 to sell design/remodel services to consumers.

My partner, an architect, was older and wiser, but our start was disastrous. We were working with the client, and I trusted in verbal agreements too much. I had never had to explain to a customer what we were doing, and now that lack of experience was a real business problem. I thought back to an elderly, eccentric teacher I had once had who kept saying, "If you want to be terrific, you have to be specific," and I understood that this was what I needed.

Doubletree Construction was a design/build firm from the beginning (Figure 8-5) because my partner then (now gone) was an architect. We didn't know we

When my architect/partner left, I dropped back to providing schematic plans to the customer and filled in the blanks with change orders. It soon became apparent that I needed to be much more specific.

Figure 8-5. Letterhead Conveys Design/Build Niche

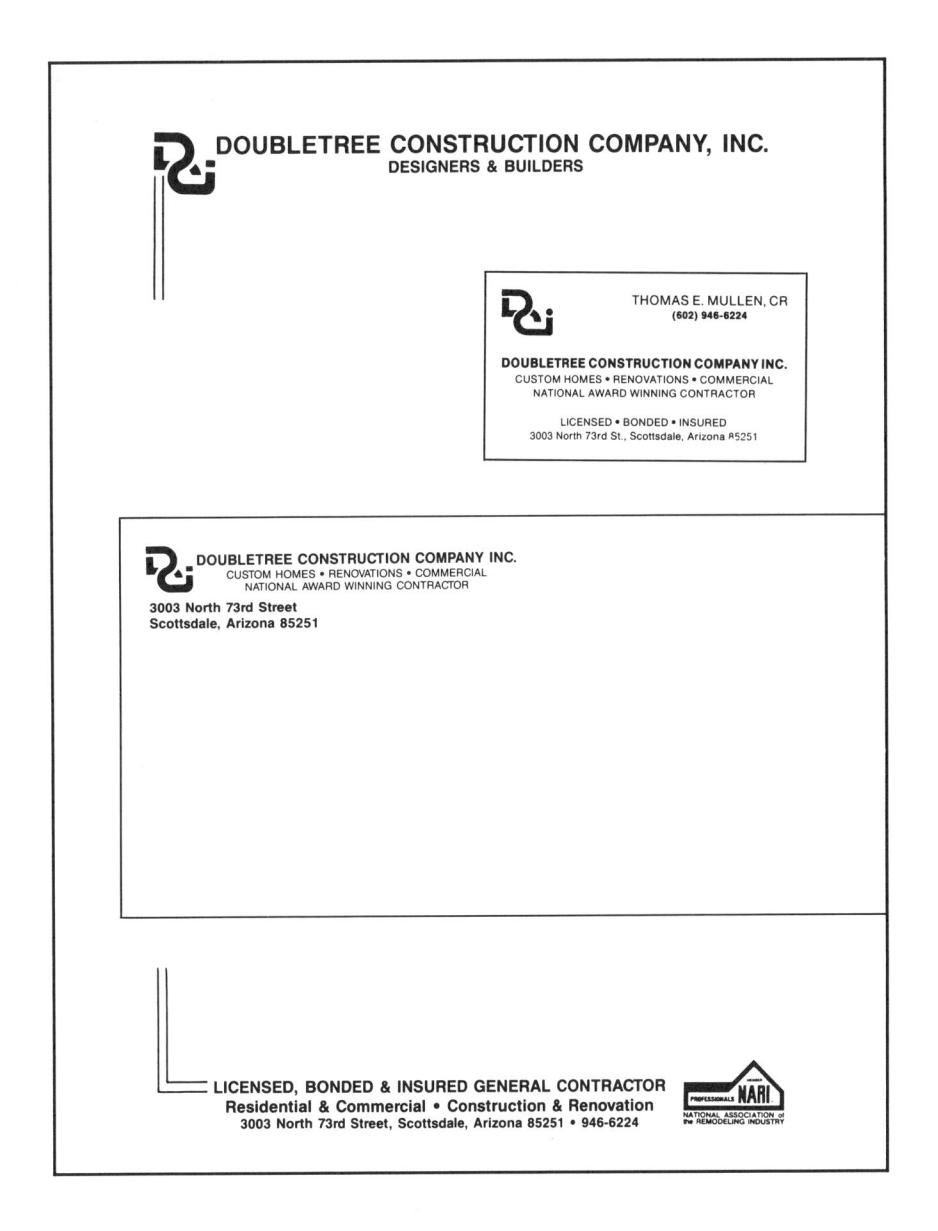

In addition I was being bedeviled by "shoppers," who monopolized the company's selling time but didn't buy. I knew I had to charge for the drawings. After all, if I couldn't get the customer to pay for the plans, I knew I couldn't get them to sign a construction contract. So I started to change.

Subcontracting Design

I brought in designers to work in-house, but getting the plans done seemed to take forever. At this time, I had over 30 employees in various divisions, and I found the cost/value ratio getting poorer in all areas.

Now we subcontract the design. I can send my clients to a number of types of designers—from the draftsperson to the full-fledged architect. I actually pay out all of the design fee to the subcontractor. Design is not a profit center for us. It's a sales tool.

I stay closely involved in the design process so that I assure that the project gets properly designed within budget. I simply refuse to "trap" the client into using Doubletree for construction by playing refund games with the design money. I don't refund the design fee if the customer uses Doubletree for construction. I tell my clients they're too smart to believe that that is a true refund and that they actually get their design free. Nevertheless, we build 85 percent of the jobs we design.

The Design/Build Process

When prospective leads call Doubletree, I always do the qualifying by phone myself. I want to know the sources of the leads, where the prospects live. I talk to them for about 15 minutes—always trying to learn about their sense of quality, price, and taste or style. I also set what I call the ground rules at this time:

- I don't make nighttime appointments. I will meet early in the morning or up to 5 p.m. in the afternoon or on Saturdays. I make clear that this is a serious project, that I'm a professional, and that it is worth some time set aside by the potential clients.
- I also make clear that I'm an educated, intelligent team member in the development of the project. I'm not embarrassed to let the client know that I have college degrees and am a nationally certified remodeler, and that Doubletree has won a number of national awards. I am just plain shameless about name-dropping (client names) to establish some connection with the potential client.
- I am looking for clients, not jobs. A good client will represent many remodeling jobs and referrals over 20 years, and I'm positioning myself for a long-term relationship. This emphasis is a subtle but extremely important shift from focusing on projects.

The First Visit

This emphasis on client rather than project shows clearly in our approach to the first visit. I go in without a tape measure. I don't want to be looking at inches. I want to look at scope. I'm all ears, and I really emphasize listening during this phase. I try not to take many notes because I believe that it hampers my listening skills. I'm looking at the client's present lifestyle. I want to view the entire house, not just where the client believes the space problem is. I ask about family size and needs.

I'm selling everything—carpet, appliances, etc. My aim is to become the family's advisor. Thus, I bid everything connected to the job, such as wallpaper or carpet, into the basic job. Once we have a client, we'll do everything for that client. If they have rental properties, we'll take care of the repairs.

On this first visit, I talk to the prospects about our process and how we split up design and construction. I don't like the normal design/build contract, which obligates the customer to construction too tightly. I give them a budget range. I don't push at this meeting because I want the client to call me and say, "We're ready to go into design"—that way they're committed.

The Design Phase

The client's design contract is with Doubletree even though we are subcontracting the design. We charge to do as-built drawings as well as for the new remodeling design, and they both are the owner's property. Our charges are less than they will pay for an architect, and I believe that our customers get better value with Doubletree.

On a $100,000 project, the client will average 6 weeks to 6 months in design. We're happy to take as long as the client needs, and we let the customer pace the work. The as-builts might take a week. Then a preliminary design might take another week.

Final design and working drawings could be produced within 2 to 3 weeks but could take as long as 6 months.

Construction

I want that design to be buildable. When I used to get architect's plans for which I had no input, I never knew what was left out. After we've been through our design process, I understand that job better than anyone else. We don't want changes caused by omissions—only changes for new items requested by the homeowner. We work hard to have everything spelled out on the drawings and as little as possible written in the contract because that's the best way to communicate with the field personnel who will do the construction.

I have four working foremen, and I add to our personnel when needed in a number of ways. I use an excellent temporary employee company and can get field personnel who are intelligent, skilled craftspeople.

In addition, our chapter of the National Association of the Remodeling Industry (NARI), of which I am currently president, has a fairly formalized field-personnel loan program. The loaned carpenter or helper stays on the original employer's payroll, and the borrowing company pays a flat hourly labor figure to the employer for the use of that employee. That flat hourly rate includes the direct pay plus the labor burden plus $1 to $2 for the employer.

Markup

We work on a 45 percent markup of job costs. I prefer to work on a cost plus basis at this markup. On cost plus, I invoice weekly against a retainer, so I am always even or ahead financially with the customer. We call all our first payments a retainer, and we often tie phase payments to "working days," meaning days the job is actually worked. Crews are on a 4-day week and 10-hour day.

Marketing

Our Phoenix market is down and has been for the last few years, so Doubletree's volume is down nearly 50 percent. Referrals are our greatest source of leads, including referrals from suppliers. We had an ad in the *Yellow Pages*, and it produced leads—but they were poor-quality leads, so we've dropped that advertising.

We do limited public promotion despite the fact that we've won a number of national design and construction awards for photogenic projects. We received free reprints of an article about our latest award, which was published by a trade magazine, and have used them in a direct mail campaign. We are also currently negotiating a local radio show, but we want to be sure it will be directed at our prime, well-to-do client and not the customer in need of home maintenance and repair.

The Future

I now look at 130 to 140 potential projects a year to get 30 to 40 jobs. I want to look at 20 projects to get 10 jobs. Our specialty will be large scale remodelings with an important design element (Figure 8-6).

Note

1. *1987 Profile of the Remodeler and His Industry* (Washington, D.C.: National Association of Home Builders, 1987), p. 49.

Figure 8-6. The Mullen Philosophy

- Stress teamwork—with clients, with subcontractors, with employees.
- Don't be afraid of client name-dropping to establish connections with new clients.
- Look for the long-term client relationship, not just the next job.
- Remember that the professional client for whom Doubletree does a residential job may be a candidate for commercial remodeling.
- Subcontract design to match the designer to the client and project.
- Stay involved with cost control during the design phase.
- Be straightforward about charging for design. Clients are too smart to believe they are receiving a "refund" toward construction.
- Specify as much as possible right on the blueprints because that is the best way to communicate with the field personnel.

9

Design/Build for Custom Home Builders

Design/build has liberated the custom home builder as it has the remodeler. While custom homebuilding claims no recorded history, probably some companies always were able to provide both construction and design. However, they were likely to "throw in" that design free of charge to move the client into construction.

In the last two decades custom builders have professionalized those design services and charged for them separately as a value-added service to the client. Custom builders no longer must wait for clients to ask for bids after another company has already designed the home. Price also is no longer the only criteria by which they are judged.

Providing the entire package of services needed by the custom home client allows the custom home builder full control of budget, lot/site selection, client material choices, and buildability of plans. Design/build allows both parties a long period of working together in the upbeat design stage before the nitty gritty of actual construction hits.

Design/build means custom home builders no longer have to compete on price. In fact, it takes many companies out of competitive bidding altogether. Because the client agrees to the budget in the early stages, as long as the integrity of that budget is rigorously maintained, the client has no reason to leave the builder or to bid out the project. Instead, as soon as the design is complete, the client is usually anxious to move into construction.

Many custom builders also are remodelers. Once design/build is the builder's service mode, including remodeling as an additional service is an easier move with design/build than without it. Custom builders diversifying into remodeling need to investigate normal remodeling markup. It tends to be higher than custom home markup because of the smaller average job size, the increased customer service, and the additional costs and risks inherent in the clients' residing on the jobsites.

Each design/build custom home builder has developed his/her own set of systems. No two are alike as the following three interviews show. Often design/builders who show strength in one particular area may be laid back or less skillful in other areas. These interviews are meant to flesh out theory with reality. These three companies are an amalgamation of what should be done in design/build, what works, and the idiosyncracies of each builder's experiences in the field. Together, they demonstrate that certain critical principles seem to be universal when custom builders are successful (Figure 9-1).

Figure 9-1. Characteristics of Successful Design/Build Custom Builders

- The builder enjoys the intensive client interaction inherent in this type of building.
- The builder wants to build one-of-a-kind luxury housing.
- The builder has a strong sense of design whether or not he/she actually does the design itself.
- The builder keeps the client's budget paramount. If the client's decisions made throughout design keep exceeding the budget, the client is kept up-to-date, educated about costs, and given the option of increasing the budget or dropping the item that is causing the overrun.
- The builder has a strong service orientation and often continues to work personally with the clients. The company provides built-in accessibility for the client to reach the builder throughout the design/construction process.

An Interview with Tony Calvis

Company Profile

Business: Custom home builder and remodeler
Years in business: 5
1989 volume: Custom homes, $650,000
Remodeling, $200,000
Number of 1989 jobs: Custom homes, 3
Remodeling, 4
Average job size: Custom homes, $300,000
Remodeling, $50,000
Personnel:
  Office—Owner plus 1 architectural designer and 1 office manager
  Field—1 working foreman (for remodeling)

Figure 9-2. Tony Calvis, president of A. G. Calvis Construction Company, Phoenix, Arizona.

Company History

My training was as a frame carpenter. I spent 8 years working with my nail bags on. When I decided to start my own business, I did it cautiously. My wife, Cheryl, was working full time, and we didn't have any children. So I kept working at the framing company in the mornings for 4 to 6 hours; then I would take off and work on my own business afternoons and evenings. I did that for 6 months as a transition to make sure the construction company was viable.

From the beginning, my wife helped to make the company professional. We were working out of our home, and she would work 8 hours at her job, then come home and pitch in at our business. After about 2 years we were finally able to have her become our full-time office manager.

Why Design/Build?

I didn't know of any other custom building company in our area offering professional and competent design services then (Figure 9-3). Some companies might use a part-time draftsperson or have an alliance with an outside architect or architectural designer. But whenever I worked with outside architects, it was obvious that they didn't have any motivation to make the house easy to build or cost effective.

By chance, I commissioned Gary Wyant—now my in-house architectural designer but then an independent—to design a spec house we were to build. He produced a set of plans that were clear and well detailed. Also that house and two subsequent "specs" he designed all sold quickly. I brought him on board, and we became a design/build firm. If I was going to be in this business, I wanted to be the best. Obviously, having excellent architectural design and clear working drawings was the most important step I had to take.

Design/build lets us keep control of the customer and job since everything is done in house. Many architects have trouble meeting the customer's budget. We come much closer. I work hand-in-hand with Gary. We pick each other's brain. This cost control comes from experience.

I attend most of the design meetings with Gary and that develops client trust. A job can not only be underdetailed, it can be overdetailed as well. For instance, an architect may specify a way to build that is more expensive than the way the carpenter might choose. The years I spent with large production

Figure 9-3. The Stationery Package Promotes Custom Design, Building, and Remodeling

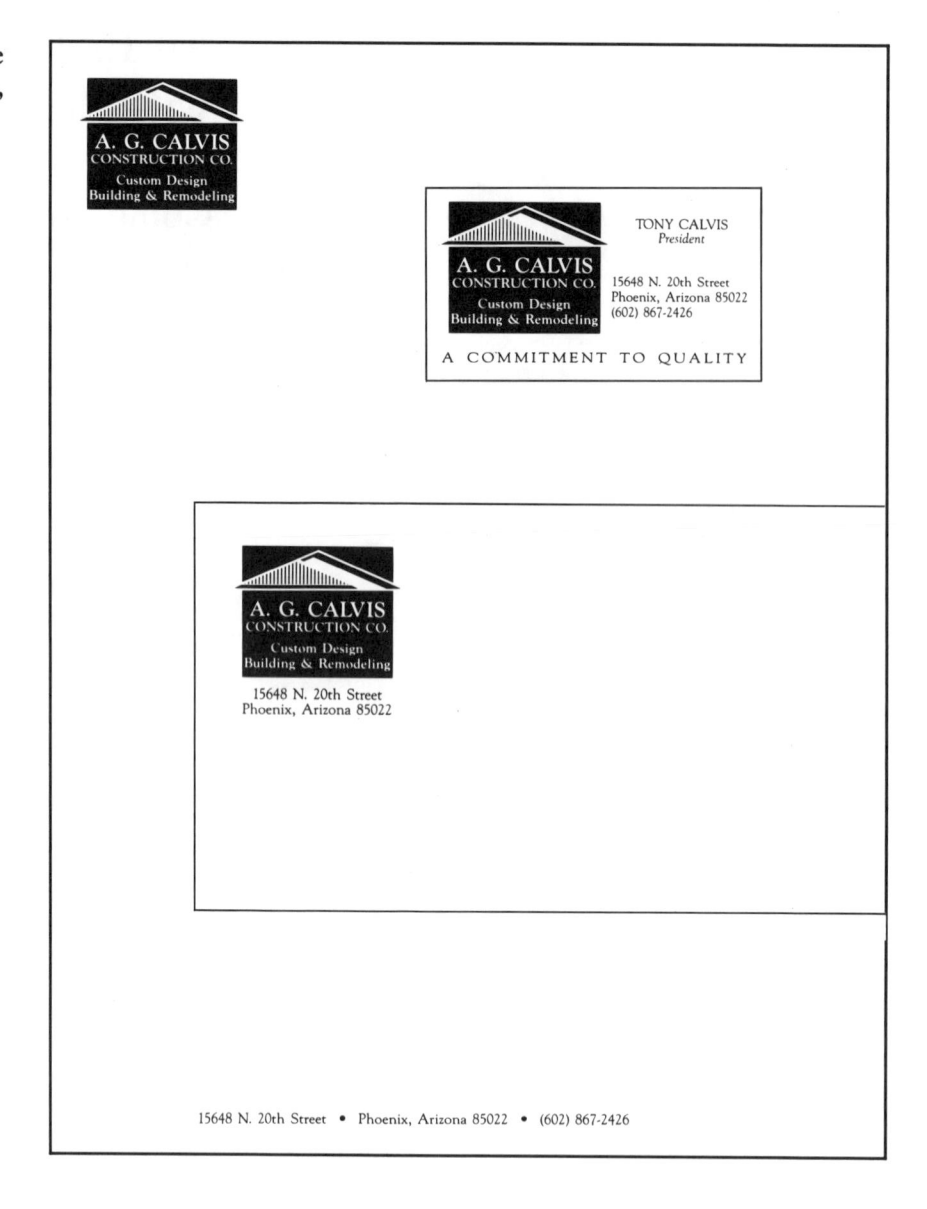

builders in Phoenix provided a good basis for matching budget and design.

Gary and I help the customer with the specifications for the project on the plans. As changes occur, they are handled by change orders. Because an entire house involves so many decisions, we handle many change-prone categories with allowances.

Allowances

Allowances are a classic problem for custom home builders. We can give a loose and generous allowance that balloons the overall job price, or we can give an unrealistically low allowance that makes the price look better. Ultimately, however, the client will blame the builder for that tight allowance. We try to give an adequate allowance and to document to the client up front both how we decided on it and the impact of changes to the allowance on the final cost of the job.

In charging for allowance overages, we often pass the exact cost difference through to the client with no markup as long as it has not created more work for us. However, we are aware that the additional dollar amount will affect our overhead costs and also that we are now warranting a more expensive product.

Customer Relationships

A custom-built house or a large remodel is a long-term project. Comfortable builder-designer-client working relationships need to be established and maintained. Our customers feel comfortable with us and trust us.

Their greatest fear is not getting their money's worth, and that fear may send them for other bids.

We've learned to establish trust and confidence in a number of ways. Probably our greatest emphasis is on education—keeping the customer up-to-date on what is happening. Just today we had an error on a job. We could fudge around the problem, and probably the client would never find out. Rather than risk that, however, we choose to explain the problem and discuss the solution, so that the client doesn't feel taken for granted or cheated.

Marketing

Customer referrals, of course, are an important source of our leads. We've been in business long enough now that our reputation for good design, high-quality workmanship, and excellent service is beginning to spread. We also find that building spec houses gives us a number of referrals. We invite prospective clients out to visit our jobsites at certain phases and give them tours. These tours are part of our confidence-building educational process.

We produce a quarterly newsletter but the amount of time it requires may not be justified, and we are considering phasing it out. Home shows are another tool we've used that may not justify the expenditure in terms of sales, but they are important for keeping our company in the public eye. Our site signs have information boxes with brochures in them. It's an idea we borrowed from the real estate industry. People take the brochures—we know because we are constantly refilling them.

The Design/Build Process

Our time frame from the first meeting through the design stage and to construction completion on a $500,000 house might be 8 to 12 months. Design time could be 4 to 8 weeks. Typically both clients in a couple work. We let them take as long in design as they want. Our patience in that phase will lead to a more satisfied client later.

The Lead

When leads call we ask:

- Where do they live now?
- Do they have funds available to build?
- Have they chosen a lot?
- Have they decided on a budget range?
- Have they talked to other builders?
- What is their schedule to build?
- How did they happen to call us?

We ask ourselves if the client's budget is realistic. If necessary, we'll give the prospective buyer some approximate budget numbers. We then send out a "propaganda" packet, which includes some pictures and addresses of completed projects. We appeal to professional people—generally they are not real estate or construction related. If the people are price buyers, they're probably not for us. We sell high quality and good design.

Our typical buyers want to be confident that the builder they have hired is going to do the job just right.

The First Meeting

We set up a meeting to sell our company and our services. We review our presentation book to give the customer a chance to get to know us. The presentation book has photos of our homes, our various licenses, happy client letters, our newsletter, a personal credit bureau report (which is excellent), certificates of insurance, and samples of our billing statements and other office forms.

However, just as the clients try to assess us at this meeting, we are assessing them. If the chemistry isn't right, Gary and I want to find out as early in the process as possible. Successful projects are not likely without good rapport.

Lot Purchase

We like to meet the customers before they buy a building lot because that lot choice affects the budget. It determines just how difficult the construction will be. Topography, availability of utilities, access, exposure, and soil conditions all affect costs. We're willing to look at lots with the customers and do a quick search of public records to help discover potential problems.

If the prospects haven't chosen a lot, we encourage them to use a real estate agent to find one. However, we find that agents are untrained, and we need to look at the lot with the customer. We've not had any success with leads that come to us from real estate agents yet, but we're open to the idea.

Schematic Design

Once the clients have chosen their lots, we move into design. We don't always use a design contract. We ask the customers to begin assembling information about what they want in the house—pictures, cut-outs from magazines, etc.

We start design without a downpayment. The customers agree that if the design doesn't suit them or if they decide not to have our company build the house, they'll pay us an hourly architectural fee. But no one has had to do this yet. We bill after the schematics are done. We believe this practice is a sign of our trust in the client.

After preliminary design of a floor plan and elevation, for which they may pay $200 to $1,000 or more, we move to working drawings.

Working Drawings

If the client wants working drawings, they pay two-thirds up front, one-third upon completion. We charge by the square foot at the working drawings stage. Basically, we try to break even on the design; the profit is in the construction.

Buildability

Time and again, our subcontractors have complimented us on our blueprints. Field design work is held to a minimum because the plans are so detailed. We don't want a carpenter making design decisions in the field.

We work hard to design our homes to be low maintenance. We're concerned, not just with repairs during the warranty period, but with long-term serviceability for our clients. We try to develop systems that attack those potential problems before they ever happen—for example, well-anchored hose bibs in our Phoenix stucco walls and the exclusive use of glue-laminate beams in all exposed exterior applications.

Our aim is to have the best design and construction techniques of anyone in town (Figure 9-4). We believe our homes give better value because of our emphasis on long service.

Figure 9-4. The Calvis Philosophy

- Good design is the secret to home value. True value comes with something that lasts and lives well.
- Build the best homes in town. Make them beautiful, maintenance free, functional—a joy to the people who own them.
- Attention to detail is critical to quality.
- Build a strong relationship with clients by making them as knowledgeable as possible about design and construction. Keep them informed throughout.
- Establish long-term relationships with your field personnel and subs. Train them well and pay quickly.
- Offer clients a complete service package including design, new construction, remodeling, lot selection and financing assistance, landscaping, etc.
- Be accessible and instantly responsive. Everyone talks about service, but few deliver. Clients have to know they can depend on you.

An Interview with Rick Jennings

Company Profile

Business: Design/build of custom homes
Years in business: 4
1989 volume: $2.5 million
Number of homes built in 1989: 10
Average job size: $250,000
Personnel:
  Office—Owner and 1 office administrator
  Field—1 project manager, 1 customer service/
    punchlist mechanic

Figure 9-5. Rick Jennings (left), president of Rick Jennings Building and Development, Inc., Ormond, Florida, Judy Nichols, interior designer for Kay Green Interiors, and Mark Pemperton, president of Pemberton Design

Company History

I grew up in a family-owned building company. From junior high through college I worked on the jobs for my father. I knew I didn't like the actual carpentry work.

After I got out of college, I started selling building materials. In 1980 I got my general contractor's license and began building low-cost housing. That soon came to an end as interest rates skyrocketed meaning no buyers could qualify for loans. I went back to building material sales.

In 1983 I got back into building. I knew I wanted to be in a less interest-sensitive market and picked luxury housing. Because I have some talent for design, my choice to become a design/build, custom home builder was easy.

Design/Build in Custom Homes

Builders have been doing design/build for years but didn't have a name for it. We don't use the term with our customers. Rather we talk about the design phase and the construction phase.

In homebuilding, we must stay on top of the new-home-market design trends. It's a luxury or move-up market, especially in my market, Florida (Figure 9-6). We're offering a one-of-a-kind custom unit.

More than money, our client is looking for snob appeal. Often the market inventory doesn't contain enough homes representing new trends. We fill that need. Some of our clients know exactly what they want—some not at all.

The Design/Build Process

The Lead

In qualifying, my main concern is whether people are considering a house in my price range—above $150,000. Other than that, I would rather meet with some nonbuyers than to risk turning away a future buyer at this initial contact point.

The First Visit

Because the appearance of my office helps me to sell, I try to set up at least one early appointment there; many times its the first one. My office is in a mini-warehouse complex with an unassuming exterior. However, the inside is beautifully designed with awards, photos, and a professional office atmosphere.

One of my primary focuses during the first visit is to qualify the prospective clients. Do they fit our prime buyer profile? I take extensive notes at this meeting. I try to decide, "Can we work together?" These are some of the areas I explore [see paragraphs that follow].

Figure 9-6. Foil-Stamped Stationery Package Attracts Luxury Market

Socioeconomic—Where do they work? Where do they live now? What do they drive? What do they wear? Careful observation will give me the answer I need here, "Can they afford a luxury home?"

Urgency—I love to hear, "How long before you can start my house?"

Source of Lead—How did they come to contact us? Was it a referral from another client or a Realtor referral?

Budget Range—Setting up a budget is an important and a sensitive issue. I just try to make sure they are in the ballpark, so even if we talk in a range of $50,000 (say $200,000 to $250,000), that is fine. Often it's a $25,000 range. If the prospects have a building lot, the location often will help me set a range with them.

Financing—I ask, "How do you plan to finance your new home?" I try to start them thinking about this and working on it at the first meeting. It may be cash or a bank loan. If they don't have a bank connection, I do. I love for them to contact my bank because my bank will tell the prospective customers what a good choice they are making. I look for this third-party endorsement in all my suppliers, subcontractors, showrooms.

If potential clients are trying to decide between purchasing an existing house or a new one, I like to use the term, *used house*, to encourage them to go for the custom home option.

The Second Visit

If the prospective client qualifies, I set up a second meeting and commit to coming back with a quick thumbnail sketch/design. This sketch will be a freebie. I'm not trying to develop the house elevation at this time but give the prospective client a basic floor plan. I see this sketch as test of my skills: Have I really been listening to what they want and need? Do I have empathy for them? Will I be able to translate their needs into good design? Will I be able to meet their budget with design?

This meeting will be at the client's home or my office (but at least one visit will be at my office because I believe that is integral to my selling).

To proceed from this point, the client will have to pay for design services. I see this design stage as my first sales close. I give the client a design fee range and collect a 50-percent deposit (on the upper end of that range) up front. The average price for plans is $2,000. This fee allows for two revisions on sketches and then working drawings. My range for design services is $1,000 to $4,000. Design is not a profit center in my company, but it is a way to draw the client into a contract.

This design fee becomes a part of the client's deposit on the construction contract. From a sales point-of-view, converting the design fee into a construction deposit is an important nuance.

Of those I meet for a first visit, 70 percent will move into construction. If we meet a second time, 90 percent will have me build their homes for them.

Setting Budgets

During these initial stages, the client is asking, "What's the most house I can afford?" Frankly, 50 percent of the time, the final cost will exceed that initial budget estimate. The clients often know which neighborhoods they want to live in. The neighborhoods they choose will dictate the cost of their houses to some degree, but their budgets will determine the size of their custom homes. When the clients give me their design deposits, they know the cost ranges of their houses.

As we draw a preliminary plan with elevation, we set the number of square feet, and I know most of the main features. I may do 4 or 5 preliminary estimates on a home before we get to the final bottom-line price. Throughout this time, parts of the estimate will stay firm (perhaps the concrete price), and other parts will fluctuate with client selections and choices.

If I see the base budget is being exceeded, I'll break out those selections that are causing the overrun and offer them as options. That keeps the base price intact, keeps me out of hot water with the customer and yet still lets them pick and choose from an options menu. Keeping control on the price issue is critical. If the budget isn't adhered to, the clients tend to bid out the job to try to salvage their budgets.

The Customer's Lot Selection

When they come to us, 50 percent of our leads already have a building lot; 50 percent don't. That doesn't bother me because getting a lot is not a problem in my market. However, I am aware that $30,000 extra spent on a deluxe lot will mean $30,000 less spent on the house. I'm a member of the local Board of Realtors, so I can help them find a lot.

Realtor Commissions

I work closely with Realtors and will refer clients to them to purchase their lots. They will then refer clients to me for their houses.

I pay the Realtor 5 percent on the house price if they refer a client to me. That commission cuts down on the Realtor's conflict of whether to sell a completed house or a custom house. Whether a custom home builder pays that referral fee is subject to regional differences. A 3 percent commission may be more common around the country.

I don't keep the Realtor waiting for that fee. I pay 50 percent of the commission on pouring the slab, and 50 percent on closing. Seventy percent of my clients come to me through Realtor referral.

Using Architects

I do some of my own schematic designs and subcontract the balance of the drawings to an outside residential designer. However, at a certain point the client's budget justifies a more professional job. If the client wants a $500,000 home (an expensive custom home in my area), I think that client wants a name architect to design it. It's a prestige factor. Just as I have a low end to what I can do in-house, I also have a high-end cutoff. I send those clients out to one of several good architects in town.

Design Liability

I don't carry errors-and-omissions insurance. If I'm doing both design and construction, I work conservatively. If I have any question, I ask an architect or engineer to review my plans, and for $200 to $300 one of them will modify and stamp my drawings.* All of our roof and floor systems are prefabricated and, therefore, engineered by the truss company.

The Team Approach

If you contract with my company to build your home, you also receive the services of an interior designer. I have worked out an arrangement so that the interior designer handles color coordination and selections for the flat fee of $250. The interior designer also will be our wallpaper subcontractor.

This arrangement means that one person, the designer (who knows the consumers' allowances) can pull all the items together. The interior designer probably won't take the clients to the tile showroom but will show them the sample boards. Only if the clients can't find a selection there, will they go to a showroom.

I've only had one client abuse this system by using many more hours than expected. The different jobs simply average out. Some clients make quick selections; some are slower. We also have alliances with a lighting company and a cabinet company. Again these companies also give third-party endorsements of our company to the customer as well as make selections convenient and easy for the clients. Another important result from my view is that I stay in control of the clients' selection in terms of price, product, and availability.

---

*This practice is not permitted in some states.

Allowances

I've found that using realistic budget allowances works—no trickery. I work to allow the consumers enough leeway that they can purchase high-quality products for their homes.

Marketing

Our marketing for new custom home clients focuses on a variety of activities.

Realtor/Developer Leads—As I noted earlier, we do pay a 5 percent commission for all clients brought to us by Realtors. This practice is by far the best marketing we have done. It accounts for 70 percent of our leads.

Association Involvement—I've been and stayed involved in my local affiliate of the National Association of Home Builders. That involvement includes being willing to take high-profile positions that involve a lot of time and hard work. Interestingly, this activity has also proven to be an excellent source of leads. We have participated in the Parade of Homes through our local home builders association as well.

Awards, Public Relations, and Image—We do a yearly submission and have won 15 to 20 local and regional awards. We make sure that those achievements are sent out in a press release. I've cut a deal with a local advertising agency to produce press releases for $50 per event. We also use distinctive job signs with our logo, the chambered nautilus shell.

Advantages of the Design/Build Niche

Operating as a design/build custom home builder has a number of advantages:

Higher Profit Margin—By packaging my services as one stop for the client, these services are perceived to be more valuable.

No Competitive Bidding—All of my work is negotiated, and this practice allows me to charge what I need to stay profitable. It also eliminates the competitive bidding process.

Control Type of Construction—This control allows me to stay in charge of the detailing of a project to make it buildable.

Budget Control—The same company that is designing that home, is building the home, and that keeps me on track in terms of the budget or allows me to warn the client that the client needs to increase the budget or cut the scope of the design.

Customer Relations—I develop a good working relationship with the customer. Selling is the happiest phase with the client, and that working relationship tides me over the more difficult construction phase.

Disadvantage of Design/Build

If a design doesn't work, is ugly to a customer, or exceeds the budget, it's my problem! It may require a design change to resolve, but we generally can't charge extra for those changes.

Figure 9-7. The Jennings Philosophy

- Network with Realtors. Pay them a substantial commission to make selling custom homes lucrative.
- Get involved with your local industry association. In addition to the good work you will do for the industry, you will sell homes based on your participation.
- Encourage third-party endorsements of our company by networking with bankers, interior designers, suppliers, and subcontractors.
- Pursue awards. They are a powerful marketing tool. They are another way to get third-party endorsements. Be sure to publicize your wins.
- Try not to bid jobs. As much as possible stay out of these shark-infested competitive waters. Sell value and design not price.
- Know product and pricing backwards and forwards. If the client is talking a 3,000-square-foot price, you have to know whether they are talking $50 a square foot or $150 a square foot. It's a learned skill.
- Sell in a professional setting. If possible, make it your office, but if that is not possible, consider the Realtor's office or the architect's office. Try to avoid the client's home.

An Interview with Bob Priest

Company Profile

Business: Luxury homebuilding—both custom and speculative
Years in business: 14
1989 volume: $2.5 million
Custom homes—$1.25 million
Speculative homes—$1.25 million
Number of homes built in 1989:
   Custom—8
   Speculative—8
Average job size: $150,000
Personnel:
   Office—Owner
   Field—All subcontracted

Figure 9-8. Bob Priest, president of Bob Priest Professional Builder, Dallas, Texas.

Company History

I started working in construction in high school and then had a variety of jobs from tile setter to working on a bridge over the Panama Canal. My college degree is in industrial management. My work background included a stint at IBM as well as 4 years for a large, tract builder, who built modular and mobile homes. But I always wanted to build for myself.

My customer-service orientation probably came from working for IBM. IBM means service. In so many businesses, once you've made the sale, you're gone. But that wasn't the way IBM worked.

I started my building business with a partner, but his interest was in high-volume production building and mine was in small-volume custom building. We parted ways a few years ago. My dream would be to build 6 to 10 homes a year, the majority for a client.

The Design/Build Process

I am what you would call a heavy qualifier. I talk to many potential home buyers in a year but work with only a few, and those few get a great deal of time and effort. Thus, I'm careful about the clients I start working with. Out of 20 phone calls, I will only meet with 1 or 2 prospects.

When prospective buyers call or visit an open house for one of my spec houses, I ask about where they live now. Would they have to sell their present home or is it sold? In our Dallas market, selling their present homes can take a long time. I ask what kind of house they have in mind? Do they have equity in the homes they now own? I also want to talk some budget ranges at this time.

They normally don't have a lot of information on finances when I first talk to them. But they know neighborhoods they are interested in. I like to help them shop for their lots. I can evaluate the lots and perhaps negotiate better deals for them. Then we have begun to develop a relationship, and they are somewhat indebted to me.

First Meeting

If the prospect is a good candidate for a custom home, we meet and exchange ideas on the lot and on potential house plans. I sketch out some ideas. The prospect is usually impressed that I've been able to sketch something the prospect liked. It means I've listened to him/her. I don't try to put a budget range on the house at this time.

Lot Search

If the client has a lot in mind, I'll visit it. If the client only has an area in mind, I'll go search for lots. This search is on my tab. No money has changed hands. This situation doesn't bother me because I would only have to refund the retainer if we cannot find an appropriate lot. But that is why I am careful and choosy about any client I start to work with.

Conceptual Design

When we are ready to begin to design a home, I ask the client to sign a contract that ultimately covers both design and construction. I get a deposit of about $1,000 to convey the schematic drawings. I use an outside architect to do these conceptual drawings as well as the working drawings, but the clients usually never meet that architect. I make sure that the deposit will cover my payment to the architect. Normally I just pass it on.

I do a room-by-room evaluation for the preliminary plan. At this time I have specification sheets in hand and record all agreements we make. I ask the client to sign off on them. We try to specify finishes for floors, ceilings, and walls. I always try to get some sense of whether a lot of custom cabinetry will be used because of its impact on the budget. Special millwork could run an additional $20,000 in the budget.

The Decision Maker

If more than one client is involved in a job, I try to identify the decision-maker early. I've found that if the children are invited to the meetings and allowed by the parents to participate, they should be regarded as decision-makers as well. I am careful to include them in the planning.

Working Drawings

When we are ready to start working drawings, I ask for a flat fee of $5,000 to $10,000. Again, I am just covering my payment to the architect. If the clients use our firm for construction, their design fees become part of their downpayments. I am covered for the expense of the plans in the estimate.

Budget

We pay close attention to the client's budget. If we are running over the budget during design, we may reduce the allowance amounts, but we would tell the client we are doing that. Thus, the client may need to use a less expensive carpet (and figure on buying a better grade of carpet later) or the client may choose to use less

Figure 9-9. A Custom Home by Bob Priest

wallpaper. I'm not sure clients ever hear these warnings though—no matter how many times you tell them.

Most clients have seen my homes (Figure 9-9), and I use them as budget guidelines. They might say, "I really like the light fixtures," or "They're too gaudy," or "They're too chintzy!" Much of this ballpark estimating can be predetermined.

I keep control of the budgets as the designs are drawn. I don't want the clients shown what they can't afford. That is our normal way of working, but occasionally, I've taken a different tack with clients—for instance, a couple with a $250,000 lot and a stated house budget of $500,000. They can afford considerably more house and their lot demands more house, so while we are drawing the house I think they will want, I'll work like the devil to sell it to them.

Allowances

We try to give realistic allowances. I've found that if I allow 1 percent of the house price for the light fixtures (at builder cost), I normally will be right. Allowances can help to solidify contracts when the owners haven't made all of their selections.

Design Considerations

I change architects when they get stale—when I start to see the newest plan look like other plans. I don't know when that will happen. I feed ideas into the architect, but I also need innovation back. If I get comfortable, I don't get better. The same staleness can happen with interior designers. My current interior decorator is part of a group that seems to keep the fresh ideas flowing. For my blueprints, I need a floor plan and elevation. If the house has something unique, I'll need a section. But we design many details on the job during our walkthroughs—for instance, cabinetry.

Subcontractors

In my opinion, the only way I can consistently do high-quality luxury housing is by using a standard group of subcontractors. Dallas is a strongly competitive market. I have clout because I pay the same rate in the summer and winter, and by the same token, I expect my subcontractors to charge me the same whether they work in season or off season. In general, I don't change subcontractors on the basis of price.

Approved Suppliers

I send clients to our approved suppliers. We like to use only one sales representative for each supplier. I look for suppliers based on their value, service, handling of clients, and whether they have a showroom. We don't require our clients to use our suppliers because they may think we're getting a kickback. However, we won't guarantee the warranty or service if the client buys from an unapproved supplier. We also ask that our suppliers notify us if the client is spending 5 to 10 percent more than the allowance.

Decorator Service

About the time we pour the slab, we send the client to our decorator to make all the selections with particular emphasis on those choices (such as the tub or shower) that affect early construction phases.

Typically our clients use 30 to 40 hours to make selections. I pay the decorator $600 to $1,000 per custom home client plus 10 to 12 cents a square foot and that cost is built into the home's cost. Clients don't seem to abuse the number of allotted hours. I think they get tired of the selection process. I market this professional decorator service as a special benefit that I provide to my customers.

On-Site Client Meetings

On-site meetings are a vital part of our service to the client. We hold five fairly formal meetings:

- Once the walls are standing—to make sure it "feels" right to the client. We look out the windows at the views. We will move these windows for a better view if necessary. At this point, the house is now in three dimensions. If a client has trouble reading blueprints (and most do), we can still make changes at this point.
- Prior to ordering cabinets. The client and I attend three meetings about an hour apart. The first is with the interior door suppliers and for the client to verify the types of doors and swings. The second is with the cabinetmaker. In our Dallas market, cabinets are custom-made locally, so we have the luxury of settling on the cabinetry details with the client at this point. The third meeting is with the electrician to set switches and light locations.
- Prior to bricking. The client and I meet with the bricklayer at this time because Dallas homes often include highly intricate brick patterns, and these patterns are worked out on the job.
- At the start of trim carpentry. We review the profile of all moldings with the trim salesperson. We also review how all closets will be outfitted and any paneling details.
- At the start of painting. The painter will already have painted 2-foot-square samples of the client's paint selections on the walls, and we review them for approval as well as to check out any stain samples.

Client Job Visits

While many custom builders resent clients just dropping by their jobsites, we welcome them. I find they often set a pattern as to when they'll come by, and I'll try to meet them whenever possible. However, we do insist that all their contact and conversations must be with me and that they must not talk to the subcontractors. We make this absolutely clear.

Client Changes

I try to attack changes in a number of ways. I look historically at the types of things people change that they might not clearly understand. I try to head these off with prevention. If we do a careful and precise job in design, we should be able to prevent a number of changes. My numerous meetings with the client at the various job stages tend to group selections and avoid changes.

Lastly, I try to build into the contract a small ($1,000 to $2,000) cushion that will absorb the small changes. If that cushion is used up, I rebuild it on the next large change. That way, I don't have to "nickel and dime" the customer. I don't charge for the small changes nor for any change for which I am not charged by my supplier or subcontractor. I do have to be sure to include material tax on changes as well as the Realtor's commission of 3 to 6 percent, if applicable. In some areas of the country, the commission is paid only on the base price. In others it includes the full and final billing amount as shown at closing.

Marketing

I have worked with Kristelle Peterson, a public relations expert, for a number of years. She has helped design our logo, our image, our brochures, advertising, and award entries. This professional assistance pays off. Through her, we've gotten extensive press coverage, including an article in *Professional Builder*. This article and other public relations activities attract both prospective buyers and professional referrers, such as real estate agents.

Referrals are another steady source of clients. In one instance, I built three homes for the same family. In another, the couple for whom I built a home divorced, and I built a custom home for each of the former spouses and their new spouses.

I offer Realtors a 3-percent commission if they bring a client to me. I pay that commission at closing—not at the end of construction. However, Realtor referrals never have really taken off for me. I think Realtors would much rather sell an existing home.

Having a spec home on the market that a potential custom home client can see and touch is a marketing tool that produces results. I also find that if I build that spec home as though it were a custom home, I can often sell it quickly. If I've sold a couple of custom homes off a spec house, I'll push to move it before it gets stale on the market.

Client Gifts

We give each of our clients a gift at closing. It might be a green plant, an envelope embosser with the new address, or notepads with the new address. My wife and I also take them to dinner

---

Figure 9-10. The Priest Philosophy

- You're building the clients' homes not yours. Don't tell them what they can and can't do in their own homes. Don't try to impose your tastes on them. This attitude is the true difference between the custom home builder and the customizing builder or the tract builder.
- The client is relying on you. When a mistake or problem occurs on the job, be sure to notify the client, before the client finds out from another source.
- Mistakes are part of the business. Admit them and be sure to develop and maintain a strong basis of good relations to make them easier to resolve.
- Be available to the client. (I am always reachable within 2 hours.) Continue to be available after the closing.
- Stay calm. Discuss any items in dispute. Discuss any items likely to be misunderstood. Adjust contracts and specification sheets for clarification.
- Identify cost overruns early. No one likes surprises. Use change orders to document and remind the owners of their expenditures.

10

Residential Design/Build for Architects

In the 1980s a small, but increasing, number of architects ventured into residential design/build. In fact, until the mid-1970s the American Institute of Architects prohibited architects from both designing and building. At the 1978 AIA Convention, the Institute voted and only narrowly passed a 3-year experiment allowing design/build by architects.

The AIA was forced to abandon its code of ethics by a 1980 antitrust case. The new code of ethics does not raise the issue of design/build, but an informal understanding holds that design/build by architects is acceptable. A 1989 AIA survey shows that 10 to 12 percent of architects are now engaged in design/build—with large firms only somewhat more likely to be involved in design/build than small firms. This percentage is lowest in the Pacific Northwest and highest in the East Central regions.

Architects bring strong design skills and, invariably, a wide variety of construction skills to the design/build table. Frequently they, like the remodeler and custom home builder, are astonished at the business management time and skills needed to run a design/build business professionally.

They are attracted by the chance to control the entire construction process from initial concept to the smallest of final detailing decisions. Some are attracted as well by the potential dollars to be earned from providing additional services to an existing client.

Design/build businesses owned by architects are frequently characterized by a stronger focus on design (as might be expected) as well as emphasis on design as not just a "feed in" to construction but as an important end in itself.

Many architect-owned companies use design as a profit center. In contrast to other design/build companies, they are happy and eager to perform design-only jobs if that is requested by the client. However, because the company overhead is spread over a larger base, their design services sometimes run less than the going rate for architects in their areas.

Because of this willingness to do design-only work, architects seldom pressure their clients to commit to construction before the design phase is complete. Even so, they have a conversion-to-construction rate equal to those of companies that do insist on that commitment. They are less likely than builders entering design/build to rebate all or part of the design fees as an incentive to signing a construction contract. Because of their professional design training, schematic drawings (as can be seen throughout this book) frequently are created as superior selling tools for the architect design/builder.

In settling on a design process that works, architects often adhere to the traditional three stages of design—conceptual design, design development, and working drawings. Architects are more likely than remodelers and home builders to carry errors- and-omission insurance. Some keep their design services under a separate company from their construction services to limit design liability even further.

The two following interviews with architects who have design/build businesses bring actual business practice to the table of design/build theory. These successful design/builders are the pioneers in design/build for architects. They had no road map to follow, no book of theory. Much of what they do is to be emulated. Do they represent ideal and textbook systems? No, even pioneers have room for improvement.

An Interview with John Cable, AIA

Company Profile

Business: Design/build residential and commercial remodeling and new construction
Years in business: 3
1989 volume: $1.2 million
Number of construction jobs in 1989: 8
Average job size: $150,000
Personnel:
  Office—Owner plus 1 administrative assistant, 1 bookkeeper, 2 architects
  Field—1 production manager, 6 carpenters, 2 apprentices, 1 laborer

Figure 10-1. John Cable AIA, president of John Cable Associates, Inc., Alexandria, Virginia.

Company History

I graduated with a master's degree in architecture (urban planning) and a bachelor's degree in architecture but got sidetracked for 7 years into energy research at the U.S. Department of Energy. When I finally decided to go back into business, I realized I had no personal marketability as an architect even though I had national and international recognition for energy research. I wanted a unique way to compete in the Washington, D.C., market.

I had gotten frustrated at the architect's lack of control once the job went into construction. In fact, in many cases, architects today even back off from what control they do have because of liability problems.

Yet, I knew I liked the construction end of the business. When I was in the Air Force, I had been responsible for building 500 houses over a 4-year period. I believed that handling both design and construction might help alleviate the cost-control problem architects have.

I was sure I could create a marketable niche by combining my design expertise and construction ability. Frankly, I thought this was a fairly unique idea. I didn't know I was part of a trend. Carrying the job through to completion seemed satisfying to me. And when the design professional is making the day-to-day decisions on detailing, those decisions can lead to both design consistency and cost control.

That's how I started.

Managing the Design/Build Business

Now that I'm 3 years into design/build, my biggest surprise has been the extremely demanding business management side of the business—accounting, change orders, contracts, invoicing, running an office. Architects coming into the design/build business have to be aware that only a small percentage of their time will be spent "on the boards."

Marketing

My company specializes in the $100,000 to $400,000 residential remodeling job. We look at design/build as a matrix with four squares—remodeling, new construction, residential, and commercial. Right now we are active in all but residential new construction. All we are waiting for there is our first client. Almost all of our clients come to us as referrals. We do use job signs and do have an ad (Figure 10-2) in the local community telephone directory under "Architects" with a cross reference in the "Builder" section. We are members of the Chamber of Commerce, but that hasn't produced any work for us yet.

We definitely market for clients not jobs. If that means doing a smaller job for a special client, that is fine. We're looking for the long-term business relationship.

John Cable Associates, Inc.
Architects • Builders

Design & Construction Services
For Additions, Renovations
New Homes & Commercial

LICENSED ARCHITECT
LICENSED GENERAL CONTRACTOR
683-6676

Figure 10-2. Advertisement Based on Jobsite Sign and Logo

Source: Reprinted with permission from John Cable, AIA, president, John Cable Associates, Inc., Alexandria, Virginia.

The Design/Build Process

We have a consistent design process. We work with the clients hand-in-hand to show them design options and cost consequences. We reject clients in design who, we think, will be a problem during construction. We try to weed out those who are illogical or irrational.

The Lead

We ask how prospective clients happen to call us. Usually the call is a referral, but it might be from another source such as our job signs.

If the lead is already sold on our company, I will go to meet with them. If they're not sure, I'll send them a packet of references and ask them to make calls to our former clients and visit our work. I only set up that first meeting with a relatively sold prospect.

The First Meeting

This first meeting is free for the client. I always go myself. We discuss in detail the buyer's perception of his/her need. I listen. All my sensors are out. I've already checked county and city records: I know just how long they have lived in the house and what their equity is likely to be. We're looking for zoning-implied restrictions such as setbacks or floor-area-to-lot-size ratio, which is a fairly unique restriction in some jurisdictions.

I learned to prepare like this at the beginning of a job after I got burned early on. We designed for a client only to find out that zoning restrictions required that design to be reworked. I resolved, never again to get caught unprepared.

I watch and listen to everything. Many times clients will express what they want in terms that they think will solve the problem. We look for the real problem to be solved. These are my objectives for this first meeting:

- Delineate the true space problem.
- Consider the clients' budget resources, time, zoning, floor-area-to-lot-size ratios, and review boards that might have jurisdiction over the property.
- Decide if I want to work with these clients:
- Are they able to make decisions?
- Are they rational in their thinking?
- Do they have integrity?
- Will they be honest and fair?

In the case of a married couple as clients, I don't worry about whether the two spouses are in agreement. It's not usually a problem because part of my job is to be a mediator and facilitator and bring the two different visions together.

Many design firms create the design and then try to sell it to the client. We would rather work to delineate a problem and present some solutions. We really work hard to understand the clients' needs despite what they tell us.

We also focus on the economic impact of their remodeling in regard to the local real estate market. We want to enhance the ultimate value of their property.

I try to get the client to give me budget guidelines. But if they can't or won't, I'll give them some guidelines.

Design Contract

As an architectural firm, we are willing to do design-only. Design is a profit center for us. We now do all the design for one spec home builder. We are looking to increase this design-only portion of our business. However, most of our clients want the entire design/build package.

We charge for design by the hour and bill monthly. We ask for a retainer of one-fourth to one-third of the price of the design up front, and that amount is credited against the final design charges. The total fee might add up to $3,000 to $5,000 for a remodeling project. This amount might be half of what is normally charged by architects in our area. We find that the design phase usually takes 3 to 6 months.

Design Schematics

This design schematics phase includes extensive field measurements. Rarely do we have existing drawings. We always do a full floor plan, but if it's not important to the project, we won't do perfect dimensioning. Again, we spend the client's money carefully.

We also do extensive site photography. We find this saves us time and the client money. When we begin to design, we lay out all of the photographs—spread them across the desk. Anytime we have a question, the answer frequently shows up in those photos.

During an initial walk-through, we gather data on all the mechanical systems without calling in the mechanical subcontractors. We record the types of systems, their ages, controls, and general data. If we suspect a problem, we may ask the subcontractor to take a look at this stage.

At this phase, problem definition is the most important key. We may present one solution to the client or as many as three. I do all the presentations, but I try to bring one of my architects with me. I'm training them to work independently eventually. I find their presence at meetings makes them more sensitive to the client's needs because they've participated in the conversations.

Their participation means that I don't have to communicate all the nuances of the meetings. And since our clients know that the staff architect is a lower hourly charge than I am, the clients often begin to work with the project architect to save themselves money and me time.

Cost Estimate

Once we have the client's go-ahead on the schematics, we move to a reasonably precise planning cost estimate. We do all material takeoffs, and we estimate subcontractor costs in-house rather than having them give an actual estimate at this stage. We will give the client a budget with a variance of 15 to 20 percent. This budget information helps the client understand the cost consequences of various design decisions.

I try hard to wear two different hats. At this stage, it's that of a cost consultant. I am objectively evaluating whether good judgment supports putting this much money in this job in this neighborhood. I believe in providing really strong service to the client. I'd rather do a smaller job today and have them happier in the long run. I've never lost a client in this stage. If the estimate exceeds the budget, we will redesign the project. Or we can do the entire design but phase construction over a number of years. If the budget and estimate are in line, we move to working drawings.

Working Drawings

We combine design development and working drawings into one phase. We give the client a complete list of all decisions the client needs to make. We want all product decisions made before construction. Color selections can come later. If we can't get specific brand selections, we push for generic decisions. Our philosophy is to make decisions on paper not in the field.

This stage includes working out layouts with the primary subcontractors. They must visit the job and work out all runs. These details may not be on the drawings, but they must be understood.

Interface Between Production and Design

I have a strong philosophy about just how detailed plans should be to help our production people and that has evolved over the years. When I started in the design/build business, we produced an extremely casual set of plans with very little detail. We were trying to minimize the cost of preparing the drawings. But we soon found out it was much cheaper to solve those problems on paper rather than in the field.

We now have two levels of design documentation that we can produce. The first is what we call a "permit set" of plans. These plans have all the information needed for obtaining a permit as well as what our own field personnel need to produce the job. We don't draw unnecessary detail, such as how to install colonial beaded trim on a window, for instance.

Even with the builder for whom we do design only, we draw only the standard details they require—not what I'd call a full set of working drawings.

The second option, this full set of working drawings with lots of detail, is what we produce if we don't know who will be building the project. In a sense we assume the worst.

I encourage open communication between our architects and field crews. We work hard to understand each other's problems and to put the information together in a way that makes field operation easier. We use both framing crews and trim crews. Each crew leader looks at the plans during the design phase and provides input into the working drawings.

We're now working toward achieving drawing consistency between jobs—toward optimizing communication between field and office. The lead carpenters are given a set of preliminary working plans to take home with them so they can provide feedback on buildability.

Our carpenters are attuned to the visual appearance of the job. They understand what we are trying to achieve in design. I believe that gives our client a better job.

The architects do the material takeoffs. That makes them think through the framing and detailing as they design. We are also working to create a team with our subcontractors. However, we do use more than one company in each specialty to keep pricing lean.

Once the working drawings are complete we are ready to assemble the contract package.

The Construction Contract

This package includes the written contract, the working drawings, and a fixed price for the job. We request that the client build a 5- to 10-percent contingency into the budget for the job. We tell them that our experience has been that opportunities for additional expenditures will arise.

We find that change orders, which we keep to a minimum, arise from unforeseen structural conditions, upgrading material specifications, or expanding the scope of the project.

One of the key beliefs we hold in our company is that as designers we have a role as facilitators. We're not trying to meet our own aesthetic needs; we are working with our clients to meet their aesthetic needs. To the extent possible, we can blend design excellence with their space needs and aesthetic wants—that's our challenge.

Figure 10-3. The Cable Philosophy

- Look for clients not jobs.
- Remember that the best marketing is satisfied clients, a neat and well-run job site, and sensitive design.
- Define the client's true needs despite what the client says.
- Be sure the remodeling makes good economic sense and protects the client's investment.
- Provide high quality work at a good dollar value.
- Treat the client as we would want to be treated. Avoid architectural and construction jargon. Keep the client informed. Develop and maintain a mutual respect.
- Make decisions on paper not in the field.
- Achieve drawing consistency between jobs.
- Optimize communication between field and design personnel in the drawing stage.
- Treat subcontractors as part of the team. Have them give input before a design is finalized.

An Interview with Walter Lynch

Company Profile

Business: Architectural firm that design/builds both custom homes and remodeling projects
Years in business: 7
1989 volume: $4 million
Number of 1989 jobs: 14
Average job size: $300,000
Personnel:
   Office—Owner plus 2 architects, 2 designers, 1 draftsperson, 1 bookkeeper
   Field—5 working foremen, 8-10 carpenters, 5 helpers, 1 mason, 2 painters

Figure 10-4. Walter Lynch, president of Walter E. Lynch Company, Inc., of Arlington, Virginia, is an architecturally trained desiger now pursuing his AIA registration.

Company History

My interest in construction started when I designed and constructed a Post Office adjacent to the small grocery I was managing during a year's sabbatical from architectural school. I took the next step toward design/build in 1979, when I arrived in Washington, D.C., from Boston, intent on doing an internship with a well-known architectural firm that designed office buildings. On the side I took on designing a residential deck. When bids came back "too high," the owners coaxed me into building the deck myself.

For the next 3 years I spent my days designing offices, offices, and more offices and nights and weekends designing and constructing residential remodeling jobs.

I started my own design/build firm in 1982. About 20 percent of our work is commercial design-only work. The other 80 percent is design/build residential renovation or custom homebuilding. Jobs are large, and our remodelings typically include additions coupled with the renovation of existing space.

The Design/Build Concept

I was attracted to the total design/construction package. Architecture is what I enjoy, but the construction is where the real money is. Unless they own really large architectural firms, architects simply don't have the kind of money available in design that they do in construction. They also learn more about business and "real world" detailing if they expand into the construction end.

Many architects look down on construction. They go through school with a certain ideal that they'll design and that they'll progress from the smaller residential projects to larger- and larger-scale projects. Practically speaking, design/construction doesn't lend itself to large commercial projects, but it does to residential projects.

Marketing

We get all our clients from referrals. We do little marketing. We have job signs, but I'm not fond of them. This year we want to start marketing ourselves

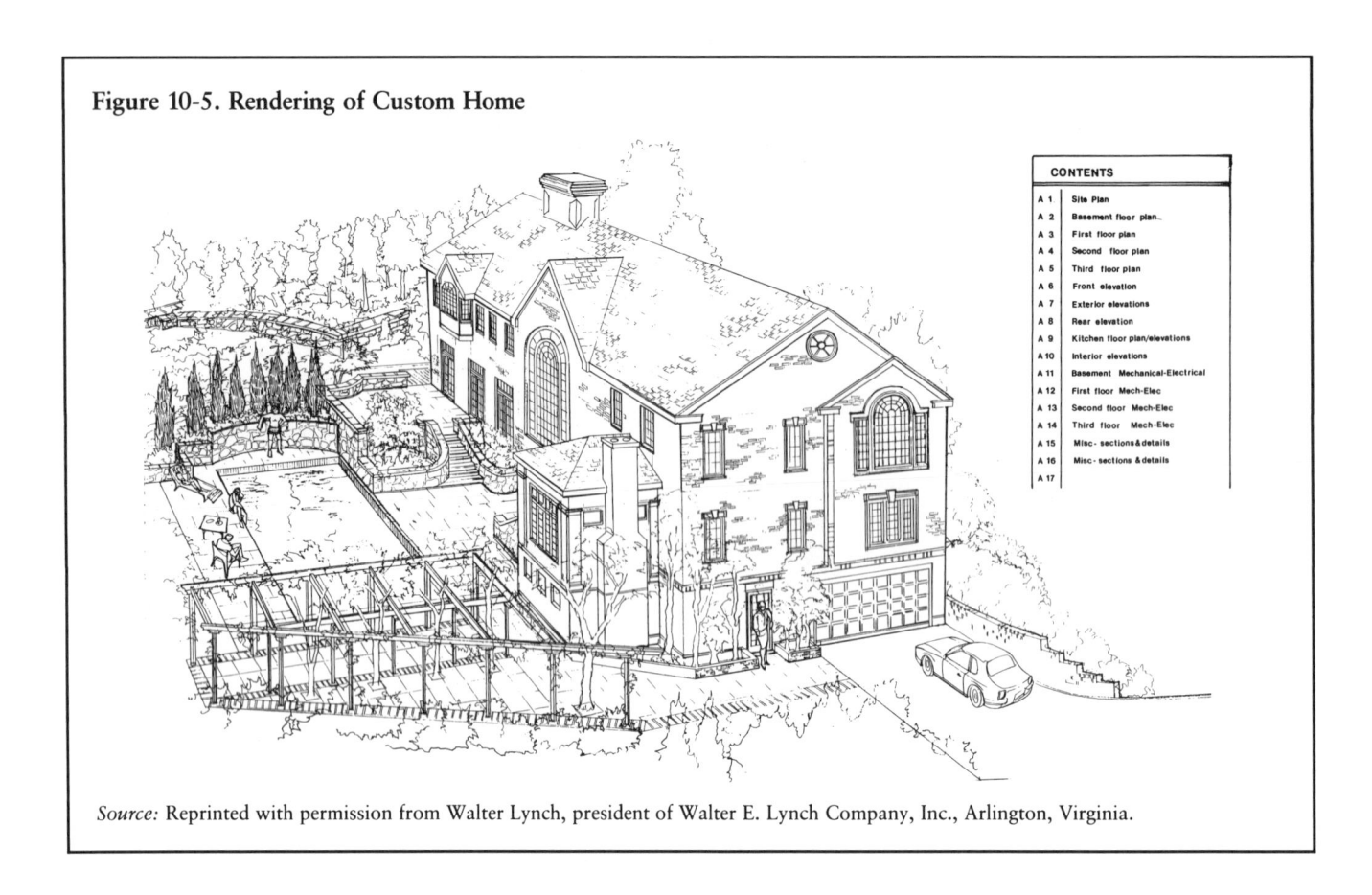

Figure 10-5. Rendering of Custom Home

Source: Reprinted with permission from Walter Lynch, president of Walter E. Lynch Company, Inc., Arlington, Virginia.

as "architects and builders," and we hope to put together a marketing package including a new logo.

Treating each client's job as our most important job is our top marketing tool.

The Design/Build Process

The Lead

I'm very loose about qualifying. Out of 10 leads that we might receive, I'll visit 9 of them. Even if the job has no potential, I can give the owners some ideas of what to do and who to look for, and our name is still spread a little further. Of those 10 leads, perhaps 6 will go into the first design stage and nearly all of those will proceed through construction.

Design

Design in our company is broken into three phases—conceptual design, design development, and working drawings. These phases can easily take 6 months. Because we currently have an 18-month backlog of construction, this amount of time is not a problem for us. Our clients pay for each design stage separately.

Conceptual Design—During this first design stage, my discussions with the client are turned into rough schematic drawings. We view these as sales tools to move the client into full-scale design (Figure 10-5). Therefore, we offer the client a relatively low, fixed price.

We bill each stage independently and always bill upon completion. This first stage is a nervous one for the clients. We want to put them at ease. We don't bill until we're sure they're satisfied.

Design Development—During this period of give and take with the homeowner, we hash out exact details, dimensions, placements. Because some clients make quick decisions and others need many changes, this phase is priced on an hourly basis.

Working Drawings—Most clients have made the majority of their design decisions by this time so this working-drawing phase is normally charged as a flat fee. This billing is also a sensitive one—a nervous time for the client. People get cold feet as they go for financing. We want them to feel comfortable with what they're about to undertake.

We are still bidding at this stage to keep the client working with us, but it's very low pressure. They are free to walk or to bid out with other contractors. We find, however, that they invariably stay with us.

Overall, our design charges average 5 to 8 percent of the job sales price, although they are not charged as a percentage of the anticipated construction cost. Usually architects' fees in our area are 10 to 15 percent for design and supervision.

Clients who want design only, generally our commercial clients, benefit from our production orientation and our careful designing to budget. These commercial, design-only clients are also an excellent source of high-quality referrals for design/build services.

Client Budget

We don't normally discuss budget at the first client meeting. Only after the preliminary sketches are presented is a budget suggested. Each of the other two phases includes a careful analysis of whether the project as designed is meeting that budget. Any discrepancy is discussed with the clients who can decide whether to delete features and return to the budget or to add to the budget. Many of our clients decide that if they are going to do a project, they should go ahead and do it right.

Buildability of Plans

We don't let production concerns impact us at the design end. We'll go ahead and design the very difficult job, but we are careful to assure that proper construction costs are allocated for that degree of difficulty.

I want really complete working drawings. We aim to communicate well, just as if another company had to build our project. One test is that, if the carpenter calls with a design question during the project, we should be able to say, do it the way the plans show. Many of the questions arise because someone has not really read the plans.

In addition, we are bidding our own designs, and we have to be able to produce a strong bid. The more complete the plans, the more complete the estimate. Our field personnel participate in a profit-sharing plan. Our foremen know what we are estimating and work with the plans before the contract is signed.

Normally, we put allowances in the contract for client selections. These allowances often include painting, carpet, finish floor, hardware, or even a tricky detail that presents estimating problems.

In addition, I tell clients to budget 10 to 12 percent of the remodeling cost for contingencies, including unforeseen remodeling problems as well as changes and additional selections they will want to make. We reviewed a number of projects this year, and we found that changes and extras averaged 5 to 6 percent of volume on our projects.

Computer-Aided Design (CAD)

We're about to start using CAD. I don't think it will help much at the preliminary design stage, but I do think it will be really helpful for as-builts and options or changes during the design development stage. Even more, we're looking forward to time and dollar savings from the computer's ability to store and reissue typical design details that we use over and over.

The Client Relationship

I have ground rules with my clients. I don't give out my home phone number, and clients whose projects are under construction must work with the foreman rather than me. But I am closely involved at the beginning of the construction project and in quality control at the end of the project. We try to get our clients to move out of their homes during the construction, and probably half of them take that advice.

When I started in business I was extremely stubborn, willing to go to court if necessary over what I thought was fair. Now I'll just give the client the $500 that might be in question if that will keep the client relatively happy and referring. But, it still bothers me to do this.

However, I try to be firm at the beginning of the job to set a pattern. I learned to do it by mistake. I had a

---

Figure 10-6. The Lynch Philosophy

- Concentrate on future business. Never let it slide because future business will eventually be present business.
- Hire people with the idea you are going to delegate. Holding employees accountable for what they do is the basis of our profit-sharing plan.
- Let employees make decisions; that is the only way they can grow. Growing is as valuable a motivator as money.
- View schematic drawings as a powerful sales tool to use with clients.
- Establish clear ground rules with your clients.
- Keep control at the beginning of the job. Don't negotiate the important rules of how you do business.
- Negotiate the final nagging problems (even when you believe you are right) and leave the client happy and referring new business.

client who was hassling me, I had had a bad day, and I barked at him. He fell into line. I've learned to set a firm tone up front. When I'm reviewing the payment schedule with the client, I don't negotiate. If the client needs reassurance that I won't run away with their money, I'm happy to give them as many client references as they like.

The Future

Right now I spend my time 25 percent on office and administrative work, 50 percent meeting with clients and client development, 25 percent keeping an eye on production.

My 5-year business plan is to be one of the largest residential design/build firms in this area. I want to keep a lean overhead in relationship to volume. I know I don't want to be forced to be in the office all the time personally. I'm working now to get the business management on it's feet.

I'm diversifying now. We bought and sold a radio station and are involved in some joint ventures. I'm really diversifying more for my own enrichment—to learn new things—but it does make sense from a business point of view as well.

Checklist of Design/Build Essentials

Marketing
- ☐ All marketing materials are informative and beautiful to reassure the prospect who is looking not only for good workmanship but also for outstanding design.
- ☐ A planned marketing program is underway and the balanced marketing budget equals 1 to 4 percent of sales volume.
- ☐ Marketing focuses on referral-quality leads, and the design/builder recognizes that referral-quality leads can be increased through marketing.

Selling
- ☐ The firm carefully qualifies leads as to whether they fit the firm's prime client and prime job profile.
- ☐ Salespeople adhere to a defined selling process and an established number of free meetings.
- ☐ Salespeople create an agenda for every client meeting to save time and accomplish more.
- ☐ Quick schematics show the client that the salesperson is an excellent listener and problem-solver.
- ☐ The salesperson asks the prospect to do some fun "homework" at the end of each meeting.
- ☐ The salesperson focuses on the sale of the design phase because the small sale will convert into a larger construction sale in most instances.

Designing
- ☐ The design/builder consults with a lawyer who specializes in construction law to develop a customized contract for design services.
- ☐ The company surveys how design services are priced in the local geographic area in order to competitively package those services.

- ☐ Design is broken down into steps such as schematics, concept development, and working drawings, and the salesperson makes those steps clear to the client.
- ☐ Design is professional and presented professionally.
- ☐ Whether design is accomplished in-house or out-of-house, the design/builder establishes his/her role as guardian of the budget and stays closely involved.
- ☐ No option is put on the blueprints if that option will exceed the budget unless (a) the salesperson has asked the client to decide whether to drop the option or change the budget and (b) the client has approved that budget change in writing.
- ☐ Costs are estimated concurrently as design is done.
- ☐ The design/builder has a customized construction contract carefully developed with a lawyer who specializes in construction law.

Production

- ☐ The design/builder targets buildability of plans as a major advantage to be gained in design/build.
- ☐ Through consistent feedback between production and design, plans are detailed to a level that is efficient for both departments.
- ☐ The production manager and lead carpenter are involved in critiquing design and estimating during the design state.
- ☐ Production constantly monitors actual job costs against estimated costs.
- ☐ Change orders are discouraged and avoided by careful specifications. However, when necessary, they are handled in writing and with appropriate charges.
- ☐ The design/builder knows that the business is a service business and that the company's performance in the eyes of the client will be rated, not only on the final product, but also on how that product was produced and delivered to the client.
- ☐ The design/builder understands the role of efficient user-friendly production systems and personnel in marketing and sales.

About the Author

Linda W. Case, a Certified Remodeler, is president of Remodeling Consulting Services, a company that provides marketing, production, and financial consulting to remodeling firms, franchise systems, manufacturers, suppliers, and magazines involved in the remodeling industry. She frequently presents workshops and seminars on a variety of topics for national and international conventions and meetings of remodeling industry associations and affiliates of the Remodelers™ Council of the National Association of Home Builders.

Case is a knowledgeable remodeling industry insider, writer, and speaker. She is the author of *Remodeling Business Basics* and coauthor of *Marketing for Remodelers: Leads for Building Business* published by the National Association of Home Builders. She also coauthored (with Walter Stoeppelwerth) *Remodeling Production*, published by HomeTech Publications. She writes the monthly "Image" column for *Remodeling* magazine, the largest trade magazine focused on the remodeling industry.

Case is the 1988 winner of the coveted Harold Hammerman Award for Excellence in Education in the Building and Remodeling Industry presented by the National Association of the Remodeling Industry.

Books for Remodelers, Custom Builders, and Architects from the Home Builder Bookstore

The Builder's Guide to Contracts and Liability
Contains sample language and guidelines for contracts between builder and buyer and builder and subcontractor, including environmental liability.

Dreams to Beams: A Guide To Building the Home You've Always Wanted
Build your business—and make your customers' dreams come true—with this consumers' guide to home construction and remodeling.

How To Choose a Remodeler Who's on the Level
Outlines the simple steps involved in choosing a remodeler for your prospects and customers.

Marketing for Remodelers: Leads for Building Business
Linda W. Case and Robert August
Attract high-quality leads inexpensively to build your business.

Quality Standards for the Professional Remodeling Industry
Reference manual of acceptable professional construction practices and standards.

The Positive Walkthrough: Your Blueprint for Success
Carol Smith
Helps to ensure long-term relationship with customers and generate new business through referrals.

Remodelers Business Basics
Linda W. Case
Serves as a practical, hands-on guide to running a all aspects of a successful remodeling business.

Understanding House Construction
Walks the reader through the basics of new home construction from ground breaking to final inspection.

To place an order or for more information, write or call:

Home Builder Bookstore Orders
15th and M Streets, N.W.
Washington, D.C. 20005
(800) 368-5242, ext. 463